VICTORIOUS
DISCIPLES

A WOMEN'S PRACTICAL GUIDE FOR
CHRISTIAN DISCIPLESHIP AND MENTORING

VICTORIOUS DISCIPLES

WANDA BOLTON-DAVIS

FOREWORD BY DR. TONY EVANS

Pleasant W rd
A Division of WINEPRESS PUBLISHING

Packaged by Pleasant Word, a division of WinePress Publishing, PO Box 428, Enumclaw, WA 98022. The views expressed or implied in this work do not necessarily reflect those of Pleasant Word, a division of WinePress Publishing. Ultimate design, content, and editorial accuracy of this work are the responsibilities of the author.

Book cover designed by Doug Anderson. Photography by Lawrence Jenkins.

Daily Bible Readings taken from Robert Murray M'Cheyne's Calendar for Daily Bible Readings. Used by permission from Banner of Truth. To order copies of the calendar please call toll free 1-800-263-8085.

Unless otherwise noted, all Scriptures are taken from the Holy Bible, New International Version, Copyright © 1973, 1978, 1984 by the International Bible Society. Used by permission of Zondervan Publishing House. The "NIV" and "New International Version" trademarks are registered in the United States Patent and Trademark Office by International Bible Society.

Scripture references marked KJV are taken from the King James Version of the Bible.

Scripture references marked NASB are taken from the New American Standard Bible, © 1960, 1963, 1968, 1971, 1972, 1973, 1975, 1977 by The Lockman Foundation. Used by permission.

ISBN 1-4141-003-5
Library of Congress Catalog Card Number: 2003107684

Dedication

To my husband, Denny, and children, Kandis, Dwight, and Destiny, for your patience, support and sacrifice during this three-year project.

To my parents, Jimmie and Ruth Bolton, for giving me a solid spiritual foundation and to my sister, Tracy Moss, for pushing me to start writing.

I dedicate this book to you and every reader who studies it and allows God's living Word to transform your life to reflect Christ. My prayer is that you will understand that by the Word of God, by the blood of Jesus and by the power of the Holy Spirit, you are a Victorious Disciple!

Victorious Disciples
Pouring into the Lives of Others

If everyone disciples one, then everyone will be discipled!

Book cover design in memory of the late Mrs. Ethel Mars who gave me the gold cross and discipled me when I didn't know what discipleship meant.

Table of Contents

Appendixes

Acknowledgements

To the many family and friends God has blessed me with, for your prayers and encouragement.

To the first three disciple groups (2001–2003) who were a part of the process from beginning to end.

To my St. John Baptist Church family for your prayers and support.

To Cokiesha Bailey, Sawnya Rogers, LaSonja Temple, and Kima Brown for your painstaking efforts in editing this book.

To Dr. W. Hulitt Gloer of Truett Theological Seminary for your critique and encouragement.

Foreword

By Tony Evans

*W*hy do fish travel in schools? Why do birds fly in formation? Why do cattle move in herds? Hyenas move in packs? Because they understand that they cannot reach their maximum potential apart from the group. Lions prey on animals that stray from the group. Bears look for fish that are no longer moving with the school. The Bible says the devil is like a roaring lion, seeking whom he may devour; the easiest Christians to devour are those who are no longer part of the pack.

As is true for the animal kingdom, the mammal kingdom, it is true for the kingdom of God. Maximum growth cannot occur apart from the community. You may have a Lone Ranger personality, but it will keep you a midget saint. The relationships we develop as Christians are critical to our growth and development. In order to become a victorious disciple, one needs to be guided by seasoned saints.

Every parent is concerned not merely for birth, but for growth. We want to see not only children born, but also children developed. We don't only want to see new life, we want to see adult life—that is reaching one's maximum spiritual potential. Maturity is the goal. Growth from infancy to maturity is best achieved not just through the transfer of information, but also through intentional relationship.

Many saints desire intentional relationships, but too few seasoned saints are ready to jump in the game. Why? Because they have confused discipleship with citizenship. They focus on the American dream instead of God's dream, on Dow Jones instead of Debra Jones, the individual; they focus on the temporal instead of the eternal. Intentional discipleship is crucial for the development of victorious disciples of Jesus Christ and that is why I am glad Wanda wrote this practical guide.

This guide provides life essentials for spiritual growth and development. She combines a Bible-based curriculum, within the context of intentional relationship and interaction to facilitate the spiritual formation of each reader. Simply put, it takes the methods and the message of Jesus Christ and crafts it in contemporary fashion.

—Dr. Tony Evans
Senior Pastor, Oak Cliff Bible Fellowship
President, The Urban Alternative
Dallas, Texas

Preface

Evangelism and discipleship should be the primary goal of every Christian ministry. Many churches have strong evangelism teams that go out witnessing and sharing Christ with unbelievers. They are extensively trained and have the ability to compassionately share the plan of salvation. They adhere to the great commission to "Therefore go and make disciples of all nations, baptizing them in the name of the Father and of the Son and of the Holy Spirit" (Matthew 28:19). They truly are fishers of men (Matthew 4:19). While every child of God is called to be a witness, I thank God for those who have the *gift* of evangelism. God uses them in a tremendous way to touch the hearts of people to draw them to the Lord. Many people have accepted Christ and come to the church because someone took the time to evangelize.

This raises a question: what happens after people are saved and come to the church? They join. They may attend worship services regularly or they may not. They may complete new member orientation or they may not. They may become involved in a ministry or they may not. They may exercise their spiritual gifts or they may not. They may become a long-time member or they may not. Many times the success and spiritual growth of a new member or new convert is dependent on the existence of a strong discipleship program. The church must realize it is not enough for people to just become saved. Christianity does not stop with evangelism. But once people accept Christ, they must be discipled to learn how to be victorious in their Christian walk. Christianity is a growing process. Let's face it. This life is not easy. There are many tests, trials, disappointments, and dark days. As a result, there must be continued support in place within the church to ensure that saints remain focused in their Christian walk.

The "revolving door syndrome" is prevalent in many churches and I believe it is partly due to the lack of effective discipleship ministries. As a result, members leave the church as rapidly as they join because their spiritual needs go unmet. Many pastors take offense to this theory because they do not understand why members leave the church saying their spiritual needs are not being met, when they are preaching and teaching the Word of God. It must be understood that all Christians need personal attention. The ministry of the Word through the pastor is critical for every believer. In addition to this ministry, Victorious Disciples will help them transfer their *knowledge* of the Word into their *experience*. The lessons are also designed without the assumption that the disciples are accurately processing their Sunday and mid-week experiences. The world might call it mentoring. We will refer to it as discipleship.

New Christians need more "hands on discipleship" than those who have been students of the Word for some time. They need a ministry that is available to help assure them of their salvation and learn the foundational truths about their newfound walk with the Lord Jesus Christ. There are also times when individuals who have known the Lord for a while may need discipleship for continued spiritual growth. Victorious Disciples is designed to help Christians move from *knowing* the Word of God, to *living* the Word of God. It is one thing to have knowledge of God's Word, but it is another to put it into action. These lessons will empower Christians to face life's challenges from a spiritual perspective as they allow God to build their character, conduct, and conversation. If you have been stuck spiritually, these lessons will be a blessing to you. If you desire to handle your problems God's way, these lessons will give you the needed strength to walk in the Spirit and not be overtaken by the flesh.

Whether you complete these lessons alone, with a disciple group, or within a church curriculum, my prayer is that at the end of this study you will be a changed individual. You will understand that Christianity does not exempt you from the trials of life, but with every trial God provides His unending grace. You will come to a place of victory in your life knowing that God is sovereign and is working all things for your good (Romans 8:28).

For His Glory

Wanda Bolton-Davis

Introduction to Victorious Disciples

Description

Victorious Disciples is a twelve-month or twelve-week discipleship/mentoring study course. It is designed to empower Christians to live victoriously. Through the study of God's Word, prayer, fasting, journaling, sharing, and encouraging one another, individuals will gain the spiritual knowledge needed to live a victorious life.

The Disciple Leader

The disciple leader should be an individual who has a strong personal relationship with the Lord. Leaders should already be active members of a local church, faithful to the teachings of their pastor, have the ability to discern and teach sound doctrine, and strive to lead an obedient life. The disciple leader's goal is to point those whom they disciple to the Lord. More than anything, group members must know the leader cares. If the leader is not sincere, it will be evident. Leaders must remember they have the ability to hurt as many people as they help. The leaders are not expected to have all the answers or know the Bible from cover to cover, but they must love God and love God's people. It is highly recommended that leaders complete the Victorious Disciples study before becoming a Victorious Disciple leader.

Group Members

Victorious Disciples members must be born again believers in Jesus Christ as Savior and Lord. A non-believer cannot be discipled. Discipleship comes after one has accepted Christ. Group members must have a desire to apply God's Word to their daily living, as this is the purpose of Victorious Disciples. It is designed to help individuals learn how to employ God's Word in their day-to-day lives. In addition, group members must be willing to make a twelve-month/week commitment.

Mission Statement

As you begin your discipleship group, you may want to adopt a mission statement. A mission statement is important because it will serve to keep the group focused on its true purpose. Every lesson, every discussion, every activity within the group, should always fall in line with the mission statement. The mission statement will serve as a baseline to evaluate the effectiveness and success of the group. A very basic mission statement might be:

> To disciple women for spiritual growth and renewal; to enable them to gain greater dependence on God, live victoriously and disciple others through the study of Biblical principles, prayer, spiritual discipline, and fellowship; so each local church represented and the universal body of Christ will be strengthened.

Goals

The goals of Victorious Disciples include:

- Spiritual growth
- Increased faith
- Greater dependence on God
- Victory in trials
- Ability to disciple others

Spiritual Growth

A twelve-month or twelve-week study course may seem like a big commitment. Perhaps this is true, but spiritual growth does not happen overnight. It is a process that takes time and commitment. Meeting for twelve sessions, whether it is monthly or weekly, will give the group members an opportunity to "experience" what they are learning. It will enable them to experience God in new ways as they learn His Word, His will and His way. Group members will have time to assess their development in Christ, determine areas of weakness, and commit to working on them. They will be able to chart their spiritual challenges and successes.

Increased Faith

"Faith comes from hearing the message, and the message is heard through the word of Christ" (Romans 10:17). Hearing and learning the Word of God is the foundation to faith. Those who have accepted Christ as personal Savior have taken the faith step. They have made a confession of faith, demonstrating they believe Jesus lived, died, and rose for our sins. Once you have taken the faith step, you then move to the faith journey. The faith journey is not as easy as the faith step. Along the faith journey you will experience trials and triumphs, burdens and blessings, valleys and victories. It is on the faith journey that your faith will be tested, because it is only through tests that your faith is exercised. You soon learn that faith is nothing until it is put into action. The true result of faith is peace. If you don't have peace, you are not walking by faith. Victorious Disciples will challenge you to trust God in every area of your life.

Greater Dependence on God

Many times in life we have the tendency to rely on everyone and everything except God Himself. You may embrace the philosophy that success comes from being in the right place at the right time or knowing the right people. It is easy in life to become dependent upon certain individuals when you perceive them as having some level of success, power, spirituality, or control. This can also be said of your relationships with other Christians who you respect as being strong in the Lord. It is certainly good to have friends, mentors, pastors, or counselors whom you trust and rely on for spiritual guidance and godly advice. However, the goal of Victorious Disciples is to grow Christians to the point that they become more dependent on God. God wants you to humble yourself under His mighty hand (1 Peter 5:6). As you become totally dependent upon Him, He will exalt you.

Victory in Trials

Jesus said, "I have come that they may have life, and have it to the full" (John 10:10). I have often wondered if Jesus came that we might have an abundant life, then why are so many Christians living defeated lives? It is because we do not always walk in the victory that God desires for His children. Victorious Disciples will teach Christians how to have victory in trials as they learn who they are in Christ and what God promises His children. This does not mean Christians are exempt from the storms of life, but they can have peace in the midst of the storm.

Ability to Disciple Others

Keep in mind that no one will ever reach spiritual perfection until Jesus returns. We are all a work in progress. We must continue to grow spiritually, but as we grow, let's help someone else grow too. As you grow in your walk with the Lord, you may begin to see the need to disciple others. As others see your spiritual growth and maturity, they will come to you with their needs. It is the goal of Victorious Disciples that after completing your twelve-month/week commitment, you will feel led of the Lord to take some women under your wing and help them become a victorious disciple. Be prayerful and allow the Lord to lead you in the number of women you disciple.

Objectives

Whenever goals are set, there must also be objectives. Objectives detail how the goals will be reached. The goals of Victorious Disciples will be reached through:

- Studying Biblical Principles
- Applying God's Word to life's situations
- Monthly/weekly meetings
- Prayer and fasting
- Intercessory prayer
- Accountability
- Encouraging one another
- Journaling
- Needs assessment/commitment

Studying Biblical Principles

The lesson should be the focus of each meeting. If you desire to serve food, I suggest making it something light and healthy. The meetings should not be a cause for a lot of stress and physical preparation for anyone. The greatest preparation should be spiritual. The lessons should be assigned prior to the meeting so everyone will come to the sessions prepared, which enhances group participation and discussion.

Applying God's Word to Life's Situations

Group members should be allowed the opportunity to make practical application of the lessons. The Bible instructs us to not only be hearers of the Word, but to also be doers (James 1:22). This is how you truly experience God and see His Word come alive in your life.

Monthly/Weekly Meetings

Victorious Disciples is designed to meet for twelve sessions. These sessions can be held once per month for twelve months or once per week for twelve weeks. You will want to establish a consistent meeting time. This will help members plan in advance to keep attendance regular. Attendance at each meeting is of grave importance, especially if a member desires to become a Victorious Disciple leader. You may establish your own attendance rules. You will want to encourage members to obtain childcare, or the leader may make provisions by having a childcare provider available. Perhaps one of the members has a teenager who might desire to make a little extra money. Childcare is important for young mothers. You do not want the inability to find a babysitter to prevent a member from attending. However, you want to eliminate all distractions.

Prayer and Fasting

Victorious Disciples will help Christians become disciplined in their Christian walk. A consistent prayer life and the ability to sacrifice food for a designated time for a spiritual purpose will enhance your spiritual maturity and growth. God is calling for disciplined Christians who will be consistent in their walk with Him. In addition, each session should begin and end with prayer.

Intercessory Prayer

Group members will pray for the needs of one another. As their comfort level grows, they may begin to disclose personal information within the group. This is a good indication they feel safe sharing with one another. They will soon experience growth through intercessory prayer as they learn that the more they pray for others, the more they experience the blessings of God and peace within their own lives. Note: It is the responsibility of the leader to use discernment regarding sharing.

Accountability

Not only should members be able to share, pray, and fast with one another, they should also hold each other accountable in their walk with the Lord. In times of weakness or distress, members can call on one another for godly counsel, instruction, and encouragement. Sometimes they may just need a reminder to "do the right thing."

Encouraging One Another

Members should encourage one another by word and deed. Group members will look forward to coming to a place where their strengths and accomplishments are recognized and celebrated. Members should be encouraged to seek and live according to God's will for their lives.

Journaling

Keeping a journal is an excellent practice for every Christian who is serious about Christian growth. Victorious Disciples encourages members to keep records of their prayer requests in a prayer journal (see Appendix A) so they can rejoice as they see when and how God answers them. It is also good to keep a list of people you are praying for in your journal. This will serve as a reminder to pray for their needs on a regular basis. In addition, during personal study, notes can be kept in the Growth Journal (see Appendix B). It is during this time that God will speak to your spirit. Be sure to write it down, as the intellect cannot always recall later what the Spirit has spoken to the heart. You may want to write down any special thoughts, feelings, emotions, or things that you might want to re-member to share with the group at the next group session. Victory verses or Scriptures you want to commit to memory can be written in the Scripture Journal (see Appendix A).

Needs Assessment/Commitment

It is important to understand that becoming a part of Victorious Disciples is a commitment that should not be taken lightly. It is a commitment to God, the disciple group members, and to yourself. A *Needs Assessment/Commitment* form can be found at the end of the Introduction. This form should be completed by each group member at the first meeting, and should then be given to the group leader. The forms should not be discussed among the group, but the leader should read over them privately. This form will serve several purposes:

Part one of the form provides specific guidelines for Victorious Disciples. It explains Victorious Disciple's mission statement and purpose, clarifies the commitment involved in the study, as well as stresses the importance of confidentiality. Part two of the form allows both the group member and the group leader to assess where the group member stands in her spiritual walk. It may be helpful in identifying both her strengths as well as areas in which she needs continued growth.

The disciple leader should keep this form until the last lesson (Lesson 11 - Reflections). The forms are then returned to each group member and discussed within the group, thus allowing each member a means of evaluating their spiritual growth and journey through Victorious Disciples.

Confidentiality

Confidentiality is extremely important! As group members begin to bond with one another, they may share personal and intimate information about themselves or their families. This information should be held in confidence and committed to prayer within the group.

Conclusion

Victorious Disciples is a study of the principles of God's Word. By imparting spiritual knowledge and encouragement, this book is designed to help Christians move from *knowing* the Word of God, to *living* the Word of God. If you are a new Christian but feel lost, this book is for you. If you have been in Christ for some time, but life is taking a toll on you, this book is for you. If you are saved, but have no joy and feel defeated, this book is for you. If you are a member of a church that desires to develop a strong discipleship/mentoring ministry, this book is for you. Whether you are a new Christian or a long-time Christian, whether it is for personal study, small group study or a discipleship curriculum within a church, God has a message for you within the pages of this book.

VICTORIOUS DISCIPLES NEEDS
ASSESSMENT/COMMITMENT FORM

I understand Victorious Disciples is a discipleship/mentoring group designed to empower me to live victoriously. Its mission statement is to disciple women for spiritual growth and renewal; to enable them to gain greater dependence on God, live victoriously and disciple others through the study of Biblical principles, prayer, spiritual discipline, and fellowship; so each local church represented and the universal body of Christ will be strengthened.

I understand Victorious Disciples is a 12-month/week commitment and I will make every effort to attend each session, as my attendance is imperative to my spiritual growth.

Victorious Disciples is not to take the place of my local church membership or commitment to the body of Christ, but it is to enhance and encourage my spiritual growth and involvement in my local church.

In order for our group to be all God desires it to be, trust is a critical factor. I understand personal and intimate issues may be shared within this group. I am committed to upholding my sister's concerns in confidence.

_____   _____

Signature   Date

_____

1) In what area(s) of your life do you desire to grow spiritually?

_____

_____

_____

_____

_____

2) What are your expectations of Victorious Disciples/your leader/yourself during this time of study?

_____

_____

_____

_____

_____

Knowing Who You Are in Christ

Being confident of this very thing, that he which hath begun a good work in you will perform it until the day of Jesus Christ (Philippians 1:6 KJV).

This lesson serves as the foundation for the entire book. If you don't know who you are in Christ, the rest of the book will be to no avail. The key to being a victorious disciple is knowing who you are and whose you are. This lesson will not cover the plan of salvation because this is a discipleship study course. Therefore, it is assumed you have already accepted Christ. However, if you are reading this book and you have not accepted Christ as your personal Savior, I invite you to do so. You can pray right now by confessing you are a sinner and acknowledging that you believe Christ lived, died, and rose again for your sins. The Bible says, "If you confess with your mouth, Jesus is Lord, and believe in your heart that God has raised him from the dead, you will be saved" (Romans 10:9). I encourage you to talk with someone who is saved and can share the plan of salvation with you. The next step is to pray and ask God to connect you with a Bible-believing Bible-teaching church.

As we return to the lesson, every Christian should know what God's Word says about them and what they are entitled to as a child of God. If you do not know your rights in the legal system, you run the risk of being taken advantage of, or not receiving what is rightfully yours. The same principle holds true for your spiritual life. If you don't know your identity in Christ, Satan will rob you of the many things God has for you. This explains why many Christians are living frustrated lives. They feel hopeless and abandoned by God, as they live daily with bitterness, unforgiveness, guilt, shame, fear, and condemnation. This takes away their joy, peace, love, confidence, and security (all the things God promises us). Although Satan works to prevent you from totally experiencing victory in your daily Christian walk, he can never take away your salvation. The Bible promises you that nothing shall separate you from the love of God (Romans 8:38–39). It also assures you that no one will pluck you from God's hand (John 10:28). Satan knows this and one of his greatest attacks on the Christian is discouragement. He knows in the midst of discouragement, many Christians find it difficult, and some-times impossible, to be in close communion with God through prayer, praise and study of the Word. Satan can never take away your *relationship* with God so he works overtime to damage your *fellowship*.

The only defense against the tricks of the enemy and the only way to be victorious, is to know who you are in Christ. Knowing who you are in Christ involves knowing and believing what God's Word says about you. The Bible says that God's Word is true and heaven and earth will pass away before His Word will fail (Matthew 5:18). We know that God is not a man that He should lie (Numbers 23:19). The Bible also says that it is the truth that will set you free (John 8:32). It is only by realizing your identity through the Word of God that you truly become free and experience the fullness of Christ.

There are three things that should be kept in mind as you study this lesson. God created you. God has a purpose and a plan for your life (this is more than a cliché) and, God wants to use you.

GOD CREATED YOU

The book of Genesis records the creation of man and woman. "So God created man in his own image, in the image of God he created him; male and female he created them" (Genesis 1:27). You must know you are not here by chance. Your birth was no coincidence. Contrary to what your parents may have told you, you were not an accident. You may have been a surprise, but you were no accident. God is the giver of life and does not accidentally give life. It does not matter what the circumstances were sur-rounding your conception. Whether you were conceived as a result of rape, incest, a one-night stand, or out of wedlock, God gave you life. Just as God intentionally created Adam and Eve, He also inten-tionally created you.

GOD HAS A PURPOSE AND A PLAN FOR YOUR LIFE

Not only did God create you, but He also created you with a specific purpose and plan for your life. When the potter sits down at the wheel, he has a specific purpose and plan for the clay. He has a distinct picture in his mind of what he desires to create. When God created you, He had a vivid picture in His mind of what He desired for you. God told Jeremiah, "Before I formed you in the womb I knew you, before you were born I set you apart; I appointed you as a prophet to the nations" (Jeremiah 1:5). In other words, Jeremiah's steps had been ordered by the Lord even before his conception. God had a plan for his life even before his parents conceived him (Wow!). God also has a plan for your life. This plan was set forth long before your existence. The Bible says that Jesus came that you might have life and that you might have it more abundantly (John 10:10). God desires for you to experience all He has planned for you. He wants only the best for your life.

GOD WANTS TO USE YOU

Not only does God want the best for you, but He also wants to use you in His service. Yes, God wants to use you! But you might say, "God couldn't possibly want to use me. I'm not as gifted as others. I've done some terrible things in my life. I'm just a new Christian." We come up with all kinds of reasons why God could not possibly use us. You must know, if you are a child of God, God wants to use you. God has a place for you to carry out His kingdom work. God used Eve, the mother of all human life (Genesis 1:26–31; 2–4). God used Esther to save the Jews (Esther 1–10). God used Mary in the virgin birth of our Lord (Matthew 1:18–25; 2; Luke 1:26–80; 2). He used Miriam to lead the women in praise (Exodus 2:1–10; 15:20–21). Deborah was a prophetess and a judge (Judges 4–5). Jocobed was used to give birth to Moses and Pharoah's daughter was used to raise him (Exodus 2:1–10; Hebrews 11:23). God used Dorcas to serve the poor (Acts 9:36–43). He used Lydia as a businesswoman (Acts 16:6–40). Priscilla was used to proclaim the gospel and nurture the church (Acts 18–19; Romans 16:3–4; 1 Corinthians 16:19; 2 Timothy 4:19). Even Rahab, a prostitute, was used to risk her life for her family, in an act of faith (Joshua 2:1–21; 6:17–25; Matthew 1:5; Hebrews 11:31; James 2:25). Just as God used these women during biblical days, God wants to use you today. Yes, God created you. He has a purpose and a plan for you, and He wants to use you.

KNOW YOUR REAL ENEMY

It is a tragedy that many Christians are living beneath their privilege and never reach their destiny in Christ because they do not know their real enemy. You see, the moment you accepted Christ as personal Savior, you enlisted in the greatest war of all time, better known as spiritual warfare (further discussed in Lesson 5). Satan declared war because you left his army and enlisted in God's kingdom. Therefore, he has set out to do everything he can to steal, kill, and destroy your walk with the Lord (John 10:10). He sets out to do whatever he can to discourage you. He works to take away your joy through painful relationships and unfortunate circumstances. He places people in your path to hurt you so you will hold unforgiveness and bitterness in your heart. He plants seeds of jealousy, envy, and strife. He causes division where there should be unity. He leads you to get caught up in pride and self-promotion, which inevitably tears you down. He places temptation in your face, enticing you to fall. He causes seemingly bad things in your life to cause you to question God's love. I used the word *seemingly* because God has a way of taking what Satan means for bad and working it for your good (Romans 8:28). However, Satan desires to get you to a point where you will neither pray, praise, nor proclaim the goodness of the Lord. Satan knows he cannot touch your position in Christ, so he works to affect your experience in that position.

Neil T. Anderson, in his book, *The Bondage Breaker*, gives the analogy that once you accept Christ, it is like walking down a long street with you on one end and God on the other. Your task is to walk down the street to reach God. However, along both sides of the street are apartment complexes with lots of windows. The windows are full of people and things that are shouting at you to distract you along your journey. Those people and things are symbolic of Satan, who works to distract and deter you from your goal of reaching God. This is a reminder that along your Christian walk, Satan will continuously throw things your way to block and discourage you, but you must remain focused. You must keep your eyes on Jesus who is at the end of the road. Paul said it this way, "I press on toward the goal to win the prize for which God has called me heavenward in Christ Jesus" (Philippians 3:14). Yes, sometimes you must press your way to Jesus.

As a young girl, I was afraid of dogs. I recall a family who had a dog, which they kept tied to a tree in the front yard of their house. I was deathly afraid of this dog. My friends would often try to persuade me to walk past this house, reminding me the dog could not harm me because he was tied to the tree, which limited his access to me. "He can't hurt you, Wanda," they would tell me. "He can't bite you. He is on a chain. He can only go so far." Despite their words of assurance, I wouldn't go. I missed out on many events with my friends because I would not join them in walking past that house. Likewise, you may have allowed Satan's bark to scare you, not realizing God has him on a chain that he will never be able to break. Many Christians miss out on blessings from God, because they fail to realize that Satan is limited. Luke 10:19 says "I have given you authority to trample on snakes and scorpions and to overcome all the power of the enemy; nothing will harm you." Satan's attack is always under God's control.

WHAT DOES GOD'S WORD SAY?

Your greatest weapon in winning over the devil is your knowledge and application of the Word of God. This is how Jesus won over the temptations of Satan in Matthew 4. You must know who you are in Christ in order to take your stand against the enemy with affirmations from God's Word. Knowing the Word of God is not only crucial to your survival, but it is also crucial to your victory. The good news is that God does not tell you who you *will* become or what you *will* receive, but rather who you *are* and what you have *right now* (That's shouting material. Hallelujah!). His Word says:

You are saved by grace	Ephesians 2:8
You are justified by faith	Romans 5:1
You are called with a holy calling	2 Timothy 1:9
You are a chosen generation, a royal priesthood, a holy nation, a peculiar people	1 Peter 2:9
You are a child of God, heirs with God, and joint heirs with Jesus	Romans 8:17
You are a new creature	2 Corinthians 5:17
You are passed from death unto life, have ever-lasting life and will not come into condemnation	John 5:24
You are sealed by the Spirit unto the day of redemption	Ephesians 4:30
You have been bought with a price	1 Corinthians 6:20
You are redeemed and your sins forgiven	Colossians 1:14
Nothing shall separate you from the love of God	Romans 8:31–34
You are established, anointed and sealed by God	2 Corinthians 1:21–22
This earth is not your home. Your citizenship is in heaven	Philippians 3:20
You are chosen and appointed to bear fruit	John 15:16
You are God's temple	1 Corinthians 3:16
You can do all things through Christ who strengthens you	Philippians 4:13

You are a saint   Ephesians 1:1

You are the salt of the earth and the light on the earth   Matthew 5:13

Every time the enemy comes against you to make you doubt who you are in Christ, you must fight back with the Word of God. When he reminds you of your sinful past, you remind him of his doomed future. In order to be a victorious disciple, you must know who you are in Christ so the devil cannot deceive and defeat you. You must remember God created you. God has a purpose and a plan for you, and God wants to use you.

TEXT

You can learn a very important lesson from Paul in Philippians 1:6, "Being confident of this very thing, that he which hath begun a good work in you will perform it until the day of Jesus Christ." Here you find Paul writing a "spiritual love letter" to the Philippian church, which he founded on his second missionary journey. This church was in the middle of a storm of persecution and Paul was writing to encourage them. Paul shares three things with them: the promise, the performance, and the period.

THE PROMISE

Being confident of this very thing . . .

Paul states, "Being confident of this very thing . . ." (Philippians 1:6 KJV). Paul says that you can be confident. You can be sure. You can be certain. You can have assurance. It is a promise that God has a purpose and a plan for your life and He wants to use you. It is a promise that God has a destiny for you, one that is full of good things and abundance. Paul felt good about the start the Philippians made and he was confident that God would complete the work He had begun. Why is this promise so important? The promise may be all you have to hang on to until your destiny is fulfilled. You must understand, from the time of your calling and appointing, until its fulfillment, you are going to go through some trying times. Why? Because believe it or not, God allows trials, troubles, and tribulations to shape you into what He has purposed (this will be explained in more detail in Lesson 5 on spiritual warfare). Oftentimes, God will reveal to you what He has purposed for your life. You may sense a strong calling on your life for some particular area of ministry. However, due to the need for continued spiritual growth, more finances, resources, opportunity, support, etc. you may not be in a position to fulfill your calling. This can be a time of frustration, discouragement, and disappointment. You know what God wants you to do. You want to do it, but you can't: what a predicament. But don't give up. This is when you hold on to the promises of God. What does it mean to hold on to the promises of God? It means to live your life according to the hope you have in Christ Jesus. This is where faith steps in (Lesson 3). Although you cannot see how God will work things out, you live in peace because you know He can and will work things out. Why? Because He promised He would and God never fails (Hallelujah.).

How do you think Jeremiah felt as the people of Judah turned a deaf ear as he preached the Word of God warning them of their upcoming destruction? His forty-year ministry was ignored, ridiculed, and rejected. I'm sure there were times he questioned God about his calling. "God, are you sure this is what I'm supposed to be doing?" However, it was during the most difficult time in his ministry that he had to cling to God's promise: "'They will fight against you but will not overcome you, for I am with you and will rescue you,' declares the Lord" (Jeremiah 1:19). In other words, Jeremiah, this is your calling. This is your purpose and when times get rough, just remember what I told you. Remember my promise Jeremiah.

God is speaking to you today. He is telling you to be encouraged and not to give up. When it seems like all hope is gone, when you feel as though you're not making progress and you keep running into a brick wall, remember the promises of God. As God speaks to you, it is important to write it down. Many times God will speak to you and your intellect cannot recall it later because it was given to your spirit, not your mind. Keep a journal of what God is sayings to you. This will help keep you focused when Satan tries to discourage you. It will help you to walk in faith as you wait on God to fulfill His promises and His purpose in your life.

Discussion Questions

1) What promises has God spoken to you?

_____

_____

_____

_____

2) What do you sense God is trying to do in your life?

_____

_____

_____

_____

3) What is preventing it from coming to pass?

_____

_____

_____

_____

4) Is there something you should be doing?

_____

_____

_____

_____

5) Is there something you are waiting on God to do?

_____

_____

_____

_____

THE PERFORMANCE

. . . he which hath begun a good work in you will perform it . . .

You must be ever mindful that it is God who calls you and chooses you to be used in His service (John 15:16). Your calling, purpose, and destiny have nothing to do with you. Never think it is your intellect, education, talents, money, association, or any of your resources that has put you where you are. It is God who gave you the intellect, education, talent, money and resources. Paul said, "*He* which hath begun a good work in you will perform it" (Philippians 1:6 KJV, emphasis added). God has begun the work and He deserves all the glory. How can you take credit for something you didn't do? God performs in the lives of His children through the gifts He gives them. He has given each of His children a gift. Some have more than one, but every child of God has at least one gift. The Bible deals with spiritual gifts in 1 Corinthians 12, Ephesians 4, and Romans 12. Some of the gifts mentioned include wisdom, knowledge, faith, healing, miracles, prophecy, discernment, tongues, interpretation of tongues, apostles, evangelists, pastors, teaching, exhortation, service, and mercy (more on spiritual gifts in Lesson 9). God gives us gifts for several reasons: one reason is for us to minister to the unsaved, another is so that the body of Christ will be edified. Your gift(s) is not for yourself, but it is for others. This is why you should not be selfish with your gifts. When you recognize the giver of your gift and your purpose, you will have a sense of urgency to use it. You will not be satisfied until you put your gift to work. Another reason God has given His children gifts is so that He might receive glory. As we use our gifts to minister to others, the unsaved are brought to Christ, the saved are edified, and God is glorified.

What about the Christian who does not know what her spiritual gift is? She probably feels frustrated and distressed as she tries to figure out what God's purpose is for her life. I've talked with many women who are experiencing this struggle. The good news is God wants you to know what your spiritual gift is more than you want to know. God is not in the business of hiding your gifts from you. I strongly agree with C. Peter Wagner, author of *Your Spiritual Gifts Can Help Your Church Grow*, who states the four prerequisites to finding your spiritual gifts are being a Christian, believing in spiritual gifts, being willing to work, and praying. You must be a Christian to realize your spiritual gifts; otherwise it is merely a talent or an exceptional ability. What is the difference? A spiritual gift is just that . . . spiritual. It is given by the Holy Spirit to be used in the building of God's kingdom. Second, you must believe in spiritual gifts. You will never receive what you do not believe. Third, you must be willing to work. You will never discover your spiritual gift by sitting on the sideline, waiting for it to fall into your lap. Get involved in various ministries, giving God an opportunity to use you. It is through working that your gift will be realized. As you discover your gift, others in the body of Christ will confirm it. Doors of opportunity will open to allow you to use your gift. Last, but surely not least, pray. God promises to give you the desires of your heart if you delight in Him (Psalm 37:4). He also promises to answer prayers that are according to His will (1 John 5:14). Our gifts are certainly His will so He has to reveal it to us. As you pray, believe and work, God will answer you. In most cases, His answer does not come as a surprise. You will realize the gift was there all along.

Realizing your spiritual gift involves allowing God's will to be done in your life. You must be willing to be obedient and submit to God's leading. Many times this involves paying attention to God's traffic signals. In order to receive your driver's license from the Department of Transportation, you must obey the rules of the road. You learned to stop at a red light, to go at a green light, and to slow down in the school zones. So it is with God, as you seek Him to reveal your gifts, He may give you divine traffic signals, which must be obeyed. God may warn you to slow down when you find yourself getting ahead of Him. Perhaps God has given you a vision for your ministry, but it may not be time for it to come into fruition. You may need to prepare yourself first. At other times, God may increase the speed limit sign, telling you it is time to speed up. Perhaps you have been at a standstill long enough and it is time to get out of your comfort zone and do what God has for you to do. Maybe fear has paralyzed you. God may be telling you to trust Him and go for it. He may be holding up a yield sign in your life. A yield sign allows the other person to have the right of way. Perhaps God is telling you to yield. It may be time for you to transfer your ministry to someone else. God may have something else for you. Perhaps God is waving a stop sign in your view. He may be trying to tell you that you are on the wrong road altogether. Perhaps you are operating in an area of ministry that is not your gift and God is trying to get your attention before you and the body of Christ suffers. Whatever the case may be, God is calling for submissive and obedient hearts that will be open to His leading and guidance.

DISCUSSION QUESTIONS

1) Have you identified your spiritual gift(s)?

   _____

   _____

   _____

   _____

2) If so, are you using it/them?

   _____

   _____

   _____

   _____

3) How can you make your gift more effective?

   _____

   _____

   _____

   _____

4) Have you defined a personal mission statement that includes your spiritual gift? If so, what is it?

   _____

   _____

   _____

   _____

5) If you don't know what your spiritual gift is, how can you discover it?

   _____

   _____

   _____

   _____

THE PERIOD

. . . until the day of Jesus Christ.

The third thing Paul shares with the Philippian church is the period. He says, "Being confident of this very thing, that he which hath begun a good work in you will perform it *until the day of Jesus Christ*" (Philippians 1:6 KJV, emphasis added). Paul was referring to the amount of time between now and the time Jesus returns. Paul also states God has begun a good work in you. This lets you know that His work is not complete. It is during your time here on earth that God is continuing to mold, shape, and perfect you to reflect His holiness. Matthew Henry writes, "The work of grace is but begun in this life; it is not finished here. For as long as we are in this imperfect state there is something more to be done" (Henry, 2321). You can be confident that God will complete that which He has begun in you. His work will be perfected when Jesus returns. It is during this period of time you must hold to God's promise as you allow Him to perform His will in your life.

I once heard a story of a couple that was planning to get married. They were so excited and had begun to plan their honeymoon. The groom wanted the best for his lovely bride. As they planned their lavish trip to Paris, they called the finest hotel to make reservations. They requested a bridal suite with all the trimmings, several connecting rooms, a king size bed, flowers, candy, and candles. Six months later their big day finally arrived. They were married and on their way to Paris. When they arrived at the hotel, they were extremely tired from their long day of excitement and festivities. They obtained their room key from the front desk and proceeded up the elevator to their room. To their dismay, when they opened the door, they did not find a lavish bridal suite. There were no connecting rooms. There was no king size bed. There were no flowers, candy, or candles. Instead, they found a small room, just large enough for a twin bed and a nightstand. They were appalled. The husband was enraged. His wife convinced him to wait until morning to speak with the manager. Besides, they were too exhausted to handle the situation that night. The couple snuggled together and slept through the night in the small twin bed.

The husband was up and dressed early. He charged down to the registration desk and angrily requested to see the manager. The manager promptly arrived and greeted the upset man with a smile. "May I help you sir?" he asked. "Yes," the irate groom replied. "I'm in room 1482. I called six months ago and made reservations for the bridal suite. I specifically requested connecting rooms, a king size bed, flowers, candy, and candles. We arrived last night and found nothing but a one-room dump. I want my money back." The manager calmly asked, "Sir, did you open the door?" "I can't believe such a distinguished hotel as this would do such a thing," the man continued. "Sir," the manager politely interrupted, "did you open the door? Please go back upstairs and open the door." With that, the irate guest was even more frustrated because the manager would not listen to him. He just kept asking if he had opened the door. He turned around in a fit of rage to return upstairs to get his wife and his belongings and leave the hotel. When he arrived at the room, his wife was waiting anxiously, "What did they say, honey?" she asked. "Oh he just kept asking me did I open some dumb door," he replied. "Let's go," he said. "Well honey, maybe you should try opening the door like the manager said." With that, the husband walked over to the old, chipped, rusted door and opened it. He and his wife stood in the

33

doorway and could not believe their eyes. There right before them was the lavish bridal suite they had requested. They saw the connecting rooms, the king size bed, flowers, candy, candles, and there were even other things they had not asked for. There were all kinds of wedding gifts on the table.

This story reveals a simple message to every believer. If you want to receive all God has for you, you must open the door. You must know who you are in Christ. God created you. God has a purpose and a plan for you. God wants to use you. You must open the door and God will fulfill His promises. He will perform His good work in your life from now until Jesus comes again. Not only did the newlyweds find what they had asked for, they found more. You too will receive more than you ask for because God is able to do exceeding abundantly above all you ask or think according to His riches (Ephesians 3:20). Don't allow Satan to steal your joy. Don't let him rob you of your peace. Open the door and let God show you all the good gifts He has for you. He desires that you will prosper and He wants to use you in His service for His glory. Know the Word of God so you can know who you are in Christ.

DISCUSSION QUESTIONS

1) What is God trying to perfect in your life?

   _____

   _____

   _____

   _____

   _____

2) How is He doing it? (Through times of difficulty, etc.)

   _____

   _____

   _____

   _____

   _____

3) Have you opened the door in your life or are you missing out on what God has for you?

   _____

   _____

   _____

   _____

   _____

4) What are some additional Scriptures that let you know who you are in Christ?

   _____

   _____

   _____

   _____

   _____

LESSON 1 – KNOWING WHO YOU ARE IN CHRIST

Goal: To Get Spiritually Focused

Homework Assignment:

- Purchase and complete a Spiritual Gift Inventory (See reference section – Larry Gilbert's Spiritual Gift Inventory or other inventories can be purchased at your local Christian bookstore). Assess your spiritual gifts. Determine whether the results are new information to you or confirmation of what you already know. If you have not done so, seek a place where you can put your spiritual gift to use.

- Pray for guidance, and then formulate a personal mission statement incorporating your spiritual gift(s). Your spiritual gifts are directly related to your purpose. Your personal mission statement should be specific, encompassing your God given goal(s) and objective(s). This mission statement should become the guiding force in your life. It should be the foundation by which your every decision is made and every action taken, thus giving purpose, clarity and direction to your life.

- Be prepared to share the results of the spiritual gift inventory and your personal mission statement with the group next time.

_____

_____

_____

_____

_____

_____

_____

_____

_____

How to Study the Bible

All scripture is given by inspiration of God, and is profitable for doctrine, for reproof, for correction, for instruction in righteousness: That the man of God may be perfect, thoroughly furnished unto all good works (2 Timothy 3:16–17 KJV).

The Bible is the Word of God. It is your road map for life. It is one of the greatest gifts from God to His children. It is the will and way of God. It is the Christian's instruction manual. It is the heart of God and it gives you answers to all of life's problems, questions, challenges, and circumstances. Studying the Bible is a necessity for spiritual growth. It is through the study of the Word that you come to know and experience God in His fullness. The Bible says that the Word is a lamp unto your feet and a light unto your path (Psalm 119:105). It is the Word of God that gives the Christian's life order and direction.

There are 66 books in the Bible, with 39 books in the Old Testament and 27 books in the New Testament. The books are divided into Pentateuch (Genesis through Deuteronomy), history (Joshua through Esther), poetry (Job through Song of Solomon), major prophets (Isaiah through Daniel), minor prophets (Hosea through Malachi), the gospels (Matthew through John), history (Acts), Pauline epistles (Romans through Philemon), general epistles (Hebrews through Jude) and Revelation (see chart layout at the end of this lesson). More copies of the Bible are sold each year than any other book on the market, while it is the least read. Very few people can say they have read the Bible in its entirety. Perhaps the reason for this is that many people feel overwhelmed by studying the Bible.

I have heard all kinds of excuses why people do not read the Bible. "I don't have time. I don't know where to begin. I don't know how." And the big one: "I don't understand it." Although you may feel these reasons are valid, it is only a ploy of the enemy to prevent you from studying God's Word. Satan doesn't want you to study the Word of God, because he doesn't want your life to be transformed. Even though you are saved, the only way you can be a victorious disciple on this earth is to study God's

Word. Psalm 119:11 says, "I have hidden your word in my heart that I might not sin against you." You can study the Bible. You can understand the Bible, and most importantly, your life can be transformed by the Bible. This lesson will provide you with some basic steps on how to study the Word of God. I trust this lesson will give you the foundational tools to begin your journey in the Word. For more detailed information on studying the Bible, I highly recommend *How to Study Your Bible* by Kay Arthur and *Discovering The Bible For Yourself* by Jeffrey Arnold, listed in Appendix D.

TEXT

All scripture is given by inspiration of God, and is profitable for doctrine, for reproof, for correction, for instruction in righteousness: That the man of God may be perfect, thoroughly furnished unto all good works (2 Timothy 3:16–17 KJV).

HOW WAS THE BIBLE WRITTEN?

All Scripture is Given by the Inspiration of God

The Bible was written by men who were inspired by the Holy Spirit. As they wrote, the Holy Spirit led them; therefore, they did not write according to their own agenda. This is why although there were many different writers, who wrote at different times, the Bible never contradicts itself.

WHY WAS THE BIBLE WRITTEN?

The Bible Is Profitable For Doctrine

As you study the Bible, it is the Holy Spirit that brings understanding of the Word. "But the Counselor, the Holy Spirit, whom the Father will send in my name, will teach you all things and will remind you of everything I have said to you" (John 14:26). He will teach and lead you in all truth. This is why it is important for you to pray before you begin to study. You must ask God to teach you all things and help you understand His Word. Paul said it best, "The man without the Spirit does not accept the things that come from the Spirit of God, for they are foolishness to him, and he cannot understand them, because they are spiritually discerned" (1 Corinthians 2:14). It is the Holy Spirit who gives understanding and illuminates the Word of God. As you grow in Christ, God begins to reveal more and more to you. Things you once did not understand, all of a sudden become crystal clear. Have you ever studied a Scripture, perhaps one that is very familiar to you, but this time you saw something totally different? It is as if a light came on and you were filled with joy and excitement because the Holy Spirit taught you something. He made a deposit into your spirit and because He teaches you the Word, He will also bring the Word to your remembrance. It is a good practice to write your thoughts down as you study, because the revelation you receive in the spirit can only be recalled in the spirit. Many times you will not be able to depend upon your intellect to recall what the Spirit has given you.

DISCUSSION QUESTIONS

1) Do you feel you do not understand the Bible? What can you do about it?

_____

_____

_____

_____

_____

2) Has God ever given you better understanding about something you once didn't comprehend in His Word? If so, what was it?

_____

_____

_____

_____

_____

3) How was your life impacted after you received understanding of God's Word?

_____

_____

_____

_____

_____

THE BIBLE IS PROFITABLE FOR REPROOF

For the word of God is living and active. Sharper than any double-edged sword, it penetrates even to dividing soul and spirit, joints and marrow; it judges the thoughts and attitudes of the heart (Hebrews 4:12).

God's Word is active and alive. It is sharp and hits where it hurts. Not only does it make you jump and shout, but sometimes you have to say, "Ouch!" The Word is also a rod of correction. It discerns your thoughts and your heart and gives a reflection of who you really are. If your heart is genuine, you will allow the Word to tame you by controlling your thoughts, actions, and tongue. You will walk in the Spirit and not be overtaken by the flesh (Galatians 5:16).

DISCUSSION QUESTIONS

1) Have you ever been convicted by the Word of God? How did you feel? What did you do?

    _____

    _____

    _____

    _____

    _____

2) What should you do when you are convicted by the Word of God?

    _____

    _____

    _____

    _____

    _____

3) Does God correct you when you are wrong?

    _____

    _____

    _____

    _____

    _____

4) Should you continue in guilt when you are wrong?

    _____

    _____

    _____

    _____

    _____

THE BIBLE IS PROFITABLE FOR CORRECTION

I have hidden your word in my heart that I might not sin against you (Psalm 119:11).

After God's Word has taught you what is right and you become disciplined through God's correction, you will see transformation take place in your life. Your desires and interests will begin to change as you conform more and more to the Word of God. Why? Because there has been a change within. Second Corinthians 5:17 says, "Therefore, if anyone is in Christ, he is a new creation; the old has gone, the new has come!" The greatest work that God does in your life is done within you. It is okay to talk about how God blesses you with material things such as a car, house, or job, but what a blessing it is to talk about what God has done on the inside of you! Many times we don't see the value of the internal blessings of God, but this is most important because it is eternal. When you die, God will not care about the external blessings; He will only be concerned with the internal (transformation) change in your life. This is what God will look for when He determines whether He can say, "Well done, good and faithful servant" (Matthew 25:21).

DISCUSSION QUESTIONS

1) How does God's Word affect your daily living?

_____

_____

_____

_____

_____

2) Have you seen an internal change in your life since you have been studying the Word of God? How?

_____

_____

_____

_____

_____

3) How does God's Word affect the way you feel about life, your circumstances, situations, and problems?

_____

_____

_____

_____

_____

4) Has there been a difference in your outlook on life? How?

_____

_____

_____

_____

_____

THE BIBLE IS PROFITABLE FOR INSTRUCTION

I will instruct you and teach you in the way you should go; I will counsel you and watch over you (Psalm 32:8).

God's Word provides guidance and counsel, for He is our divine teacher. After your life has been transformed, you then can allow God's Word to direct you in every decision of your life. This is when your steps are truly ordered by the Lord. You begin to seek God for answers rather than seeking the counsel of man. Proverbs 3:5–6 says, "Trust in the Lord with all your heart and lean not on your own understanding; in all your ways acknowledge him, and he will make your paths straight." The more you study the Bible the more you will seek God for His divine direction for your life. He will reveal your destiny and your gifts as you walk according to His will.

DISCUSSION QUESTIONS

1) How did you make decisions before studying the Word?

_____

_____

_____

_____

_____

2) How do you make decisions now?

_____

_____

_____

_____

_____

3) Have you experienced transformation in your life? If so, how? If not, what do you need to do?

_____

_____

_____

_____

_____

4) What areas in your life remain in need of transformation?

_____

_____

_____

_____

_____

PRACTICAL APPLICATION

Now that we have a better understanding of how and why the Word of God was written, let us learn how we can study the Bible more effectively. There are various types of study methods. You may utilize only one or several simultaneously. They each provide you with a working knowledge of the Word. These include topical study, book study, character study, expository study, word study, and chronological study.

Topical Study

A topical study is when you select a specific topic to study. You will need a Bible concordance. I recommend *The New Strong's Exhaustive Concordance of the Bible* (James Strong). A concordance provides a list of topics in alphabetical order with Scriptures pertaining to that topic. This is an excellent method of study to learn what God's Word says about specific topics that may be of interest or relate to your life (such as marriage, children, finances, prayer, and faith). However, when doing a topical study, it is important to study the Scripture in its proper context. Often, the temptation is to take a portion of Scripture and make it say and validate what you would like, rather than give it proper interpretation. Read the verses before and after a particular verse to ensure proper understanding.

Book Study

A book study is the study of a particular book. It is a good idea to have a notebook. Perhaps you should have a notebook for each book you study. Once you select a book to study, I recommend reading the book several times. For longer books this may take several days, but that's okay. Each time you read the book, you will gain clearer understanding. You will want to note: *who wrote the book; to whom was it written; where, when and why it was written; what was going on when the book was written; and identify the overall theme of the book.* Write a summary of each chapter. A Bible dictionary will be helpful in defining words you do not understand. Use a concordance to find other passages with the same word to get proper interpretation. In other words, let Scripture interpret Scripture. As you study the book, read and study the Scripture in its proper context, by examining what comes before and after. Many verses can be interpreted incorrectly when examined alone.

Character or Biographical Study

A character or biographical study is when you study a particular person in the Bible. You will take note of the person's heritage, cultural background, the meaning of his/her name, the events surrounding their life, and so forth.

Expository Study

An expository study is an exhaustive study of the Word. It is the verse-by-verse study of the Word. Once again the whole chapter or book is read several times. However, your notes will be a summary of each verse rather than each chapter. Although it is very time consuming, it can prove to be very thorough and provide a deep knowledge and understanding of the Word of God.

Word Study

A word study is very similar to the topical study, except the word may not necessarily be a topic. You may find that a particular word is repeated several times within a text. In such cases, you may want to do a word study on that particular word. It is done exactly the same way by looking up the word in the alphabetical listing of a Bible concordance. A list of Scriptures pertaining to this word is provided. This type of study allows you to explore the meaning of a word within the context of its original language.

Chronological Study

A chronological study is the study of the Word according to its sequence of events and history. Although the Bible may be studied in order of Genesis to Revelation, it is not written sequentially.

LEADING OF THE HOLY SPIRIT

I would be remiss if I did not discuss studying the Bible according to the Holy Spirit's leading. I have experienced some of my greatest blessings from the study of the Word by strictly being led by the Holy Spirit. This is when you hear God telling you to study a particular passage or book. There have also been times when I have opened my Bible and God led me to a particular passage that spoke to my spirit in a powerful way. Therefore, do not omit being led by the Spirit in your study. However, you should not allow this to substitute a systematic approach. This is why it is important to pray before and after your study. Pray before you study and ask God to give you understanding in your study. Pray after you study and ask God to seal in your heart what you have studied so you can walk in obedience.

YOU MUST HAVE THE RIGHT TOOLS

As you approach your journey of the study of the Word, whether it is a new journey or whether you are making a commitment to improve your study habits, it is imperative that you have the right tools. Can you imagine a mechanic trying to change a tire without a lug wrench, a jack and a spare tire? He would have a difficult time. It is the same for the Christian who is studying the Word without the proper tools. Even a student in school must purchase the correct textbook and other supplies for the class. So, this means it will require an investment. Yes, you will have to spend some money if you want to have the proper tools. Now before you close this book, allow me to share something with you. I have a friend who told me when she first accepted Christ, she despised spending her money in the Christian bookstore (on spiritual things). Now that she has grown in the Lord, when she goes to the Christian bookstore, she actually has to leave some of her money at home to keep from spending it all. What is the difference? Spiritual growth. As you grow in the Lord, you realize you are not just spending money, but you are investing in your soul and the kingdom. If you are on a strict budget, you may need to purchase one or two resources at a time. Whatever sacrifices you have to make, your soul is worth it. So let's get equipped to study the Word! These are the tools you will find to be helpful:

STUDY RESOURCES

Study Bible

There are many different types of Bibles available in the Christian bookstores. They vary in size and price. I have many different Bibles, one being a study Bible. I found the *Thompson Chain-Reference Bible* to be excellent. Study Bibles provide more information than just the printed text Bibles. They give a listing of related Scriptures, notes regarding the passage in the margins, a small concordance, historical information, maps and a lot more. This additional information will help you tremendously in your study. It is also good to have other Bibles of different translations (e.g. King James Version, New King James Version, New International Version). This will enable you to compare Scripture in the various translations, thus giving clarification to what the text is saying. It is also good to have a small pocket Bible to carry with you. It may not always be convenient to carry your larger Bible, but carrying a small Bible in your purse or pocket will allow the Word to be with you at all times.

Concordance

A concordance is a must in every Christian's library. As mentioned before, the concordance will allow you to look up various topics and words as well as assist in looking up specific Scripture. *The New Strong's Exhaustive Concordance of the Bible* (James Strong) also includes a Greek and Hebrew dictionary.

Bible Dictionary

A Bible dictionary will enable you to study the meaning of biblical words in the original languages. *Vine's Complete Expository Dictionary of Old and New Testament Words* (W.E. Vine, Unger, White, Jr.) provide words in English, Greek and Hebrew. It also includes Scripture passages illustrating particular usages of words. The *Vine's Dictionary* uses the same reference numbers as *Strong's Concordance*, so you will be able to cross-reference.

Commentary

A commentary will give thorough explanation of the text; this may include literary background and other important information. It is usually the commentary that will provide the student with greater understanding and insight of the text. There are many different commentaries and don't be surprised if sometimes they give differing views on a particular text. You must remember, commentaries are simply an individual's interpretation of the Bible. This is why it is essential when studying the Bible that you read it for yourself, establish your own theological basis and then refer to a commentary. It may be good to reference more than one. A good one is *Matthew Henry's Commentary on the Whole Bible* (Hendrickson).

These are some basic tools you will find helpful as you study the Bible. You will find having good resources and the proper tools will make your study easier and more enjoyable. You will soon learn the more you study and obey, the more your life will be blessed.

STUDY TIPS

Do your best to present yourself to God as one approved, a workman who does not need to be ashamed and who correctly handles the word of truth (2 Timothy 2:15).

1) Build your library with study resources.
2) Always pray before and after you study.
3) Develop a systematic study method.
4) Be consistent—plan your study time.
5) Keep notes—write down what the Lord reveals to you. Ask yourself, "What is the text saying? What is it saying to me?" Don't be afraid to write in your Bible!
6) Repetition is good. Review your notes. It will help plant the Word deep in your heart.
7) Memorize Scripture.
8) Meditate on God's Word.
9) Share the Word with others.
10) Continuously feed your spirit through study of the Word, reading inspirational books, listening to tapes, reviewing sermon/Bible class notes, Christian music, and fellowshipping with other believers.

God will give you the desire to study His Word. The Word is spiritual food for your soul, just as natural food is for your body. You will become spiritually undernourished if you are not feeding your spirit daily. Take your time in your study. Don't push yourself. If you don't understand something, research for clarification and don't hesitate to ask your pastor or another Christian brother or sister. The goal for reading the Bible is not to be able to say, "I study the Word" or "I've read the whole Bible from Genesis to Revelation." The goal is to get to know the Lord personally and intimately, as your life becomes a true reflection of Him. The benefits of studying the Word are incomprehensible. So let's get ready for an exciting journey through the study of God's Word. You will experience a *RENEWED RELATIONSHIP WITH THE FATHER, UNDERSTANDING OF THE REVEALED WORD AND A JUST REWARD! HALLELUJAH!*

Books of the Bible

OLD TESTAMENT

PENTATEUCH
GENESIS EXODUS LEVITICUS
NUMBERS DEUTERONOMY

HISTORY
JOSHUA JUDGES RUTH
I SAMUEL II SAMUEL I KINGS II KINGS
I CHRONICLES II CHRONICLES EZRA
NEHEMIAH ESTHER

POETRY
JOB PSALMS PROVERBS
ECCLESIASTES SONG OF SOLOMON

MAJOR PROPHETS
ISAIAH JEREMIAH LAMENTATIONS
EZEKIEL DANIEL

MINOR PROPHETS
HOSEA JOEL AMOS OBADIAH
JONAH MICAH NAHUM
HABAKKUK ZEPHANIAH HAGGAI
ZECHARIAH MALACHI

NEW TESTAMENT

THE GOSPELS
MATTHEW MARK LUKE JOHN

HISTORY
ACTS

PAULINE EPISTLES
ROMANS I CORINTHIANS
II CORINTHIANS GALATIANS
EPHESIANS PHILIPPIANS COLOSSIANS
I THESSALONIANS II THESSALONIANS
I TIMOTHY II TIMOTHY
TITUS PHILEMON

GENERAL EPISTLES
HEBREWS JAMES I PETER
II PETER I JOHN II JOHN
III JOHN JUDE

REVELATION

LESSON 2 – HOW TO STUDY THE BIBLE

Goal: To develop consistency in reading God's Word and apply it to your life

Homework Assignment:

- Make a commitment to read the Bible on a daily basis (See the calendar for Daily Bible Readings at the end of the book).

- Select a book of the Bible to study for the next month. Record in your journal what you learn, what God speaks to you and how you can apply it to your life. Ask questions of the text – Who? What? When? Where? And why? After you have completed one book, choose another and continue.

- Be prepared to share your spiritual journey with the group next time.

_____

_____

_____

_____

_____

_____

_____

_____

_____

_____

_____

_____

The Journey of Faith

And without faith it is impossible to please God, because anyone who comes to him must believe that he exists and that he rewards those who earnestly seek him (Hebrews 11:6).

One of the greatest challenges for Christians is to have faith. We want to have it. We know as born again believers we are supposed to have it. But yet, many times it is an area in which we struggle. There are times we pretend to have it when we don't and perhaps there are times we think we have and we don't. Nevertheless, faith is necessary for our Christian walk. The Bible says, "Without faith it is impossible to please God" (Hebrews 11:6). So what exactly is faith? The Bible describes faith as ". . . being sure of what we hope for and certain of what we do not see" (Hebrews 11:1). It is calling those things which are not, as though they were (Romans 4:17). Faith comes by hearing and hearing by the Word of God (Romans 10:17). Matthew Henry states, "Faith is acting on the truth you believe." One preacher shares that "faith is acting like you know God's Word is true." I've heard it said that faith is trusting God no matter what. To sum it all up, faith is knowing God will make a way when there is no way.

God lets you know in His Word that if you don't have faith, everything else you attempt to do for Him is to no avail (Hebrews 11:6). Wow! That is pretty deep—to think that God puts so much weight on faith, that He would not be satisfied with worship, praise, devotion, service, Bible study, or prayers if you lack faith. "Why," you might ask, "is faith so important?" You must know it is important because it takes faith to be saved. Think about it. You didn't see Jesus walk the earth. You didn't see Him die on the cross. You didn't see God raise Him from the dead. You believe this by faith. That's why Ephesians 2:8 says, "For it is by grace you have been saved, through faith—and this not from yourselves, it is the gift of God." You must have faith in order to be saved. I refer to this as the *faith step*. It is your first encounter with faith as you step into salvation, declaring you believe Jesus lived, died, and rose again for your sins. However, after you have made the faith step, you then move to the *faith journey*. The faith journey is where you begin to trust God in your daily experiences. It is good to take the faith step and trust God with your soul, but you must also travel the faith journey and trust God with your everyday situations, challenges, and experiences. Second Corinthians 5:7 says you must walk by faith and not by sight. This is referring to your daily experiences. The faith journey requires you to trust God enough to believe in His Word and apply it to your personal life. The faith journey is not as easy as the faith step. The faith journey is a growing process. As you grow in the knowledge of the Word, your faith will also increase.

The eleventh chapter of the book of Hebrews is known as the faith chapter. It has been referred to as the "Hall of Faith." It is the roll call of the heroes and heroines of faith. This epistle was written primarily to the Hebrew Christians because they were often tempted to go back to their old ways and practices of Judaism. Chapter 11 gives a long list of those who stood steadfast in their faith.

TEXT

As you observe Hebrews 11, you learn four lessons: you must have faith in God's Word, you must have faith in your worship, you must have faith in your walk, and you must have faith in your work.

YOU MUST HAVE FAITH IN GOD'S WORD

By faith we understand that the universe was formed at God's command, so that what is seen was not made out of what was visible (Hebrews 11:3).

John 1:1–3 states, "In the beginning was the Word, and the Word was with God, and the Word was God. He was with God in the beginning. Through him all things were made; without him nothing was made that has been made." The journey of faith requires you to believe in the inerrancy of God's Word simply because your faith is based upon the Word of God. The Bible says that God spoke and the world came into existence. He declared the universe into existence out of nothing. His Word is powerful and it is still as powerful today as it was then. If you are going to have faith in God's Word, you must *believe it, receive it, and achieve it.*

Believe It

One of Satan's greatest deterrents of your faith is unbelief. He works to keep non-Christians in darkness through unbelief or partial belief. He works to keep believers in doubt through lack of knowledge. Therefore, on the faith journey, you must know what God's Word says and believe it. You cannot have faith in something you do not believe in. Not only must you believe in God's Word in general, but you must also believe what God's Word says about you personally. Scripture must be taken and applied to your life to enable you to see its relevance and personal application. You must believe that you are saved by grace (Ephesians 2:8); that you are more than a conqueror (Romans 8:37); that no weapon formed against you shall prosper (Isaiah 54:17); that you are fearfully and wonderfully made (Psalm 139:14); that God will never leave you nor forsake you (Hebrews 13:5); that you can do all things through Christ who strengthens you (Philippians 4:13); that nothing shall separate you from the love of God (Romans 8:39). Scripture comes alive when you allow it to speak to your situation.

Receive It

It's one thing to believe God's Word and it's another to receive it. To believe it says, "I agree. It's true. I know that it's right." However, to receive it says, "I'm going to apply it to my life. I'm going to walk in it, dwell in it, live in it and obey it." Many times you may find yourself able to believe and receive God's Word for others, but not for yourself. You see God work in the lives of others but you don't believe He can work in your situation. You can attest that God saved your friend's marriage, but you doubt He can save yours. This is why many Christians live in a state of mere existence. They have life, but they have no joy, no love, no peace, nor other things God says is ours to have. They *believe* the Word of God, but they have not *received* it into their hearts.

Achieve It

It is only after you have believed the Word, and received the Word, that you can achieve according to the Word. Your achievement is not based upon anything you can do. It is based solely upon the Word of God. This is what faith is all about. Because you know God's Word is true and that the Bible says that heaven and earth will pass away before His Word fails (Matthew 24:35), then your faith is rooted and grounded in the Word of God. Perhaps you have wondered how it seems some people have such strong faith while facing what appears to be impossible circumstances. It is because they have faith in the Word of God.

I once heard someone say, it is not so much the amount of your faith, but it is the object of your faith that matters. Many times there is a waiting period between your believing and receiving the Word and your achieving the blessing. This waiting period is when your faith must be put into action. You stand on the Word of God while you wait to see it manifested in your life. Faith is not faith until it is activated. I remember when I first started working out. I was amazed at the definition that became apparent in the muscles of my legs, arms and abdomen. What I came to realize is that the muscles were there all the time, but they became stronger as I used them. This is true of faith, the more it is exercised the stronger it becomes.

DISCUSSION QUESTIONS

1) Have you ever experienced times when you have doubted the Word of God? What did you do?

_____

_____

_____

_____

_____

2) Think about a particular problem you may be facing. How can you apply God's Word to it? Are you being obedient?

_____

_____

_____

_____

_____

3) Faith requires you to trust God. Sometimes that means waiting on Him. Have you ever had to wait on God? What did you do while you were waiting?

_____

_____

_____

_____

_____

You Must Have Faith in Your Worship

By faith Abel offered God a better sacrifice than Cain did. By faith he was commended as a righteous man, when God spoke well of his offerings. And by faith he still speaks, even though he is dead (Hebrews 11:4).

Faith in our worship involves sacrifice, service, and selflessness.

Sacrifice

Perhaps you can recall the story of Cain and Abel, the sons of Adam and Eve (Genesis 4) who came to present sacrifices before the Lord. This was customary during Old Testament times for the forgiveness of sins. Annually, people would gather up the best of their livestock to sacrifice it unto God in order to bring themselves back in right standing with the Lord. This was their way of worshipping God and obtaining forgiveness for their sins. When it was time to bring sacrifices to the Lord, Abel acted under the power of faith. He brought a sacrifice of atonement. He brought a blood sacrifice, while at the same time acknowledging himself as a sinner, hoping for mercy through his sacrifice. Cain, on the other hand, brought a sacrifice that was a mere "thank" offering. He did not have a repentant heart and his offering was unacceptable.

Today you can thank God that Jesus' death and resurrection abolished the old system of atonement. Hebrews 10:12 says that Jesus became our sacrifice once and for all. Sacrifices are no longer required for the remission of sins. Now, you just merely ask: "If we confess our sins, he is faithful and just and will forgive us our sins and purify us from all unrighteousness" (1 John 1:9).

As you worship God today, present acceptable sacrifices unto Him. Have you been guilty of laying sacrifices before Him that are unacceptable? His Word says to present unto Him a sacrifice of praise (Hebrews 13:15). You must also present your body as a living sacrifice (Romans 12:1). God wants you to worship Him and yield your body totally to Him for His use and purpose.

Service

You cannot worship God without serving Him. Your greatest service *to Him* is through kingdom building *for Him.* The motive of everything you do for Christ should be to lead others to Him. The great commission is given to all believers in Matthew 28:19–20, "Therefore go and make disciples of all nations, baptizing them in the name of the Father and of the Son and of the Holy Spirit and teaching them to obey everything I have commanded you." Any other motive is not of God. Serving God involves utilizing the gifts He has given you to bring glory to Him, to save the lost, and to build up the body of Christ.

Selflessness

If anyone would come after me, he must deny himself and take up his cross daily and follow me (Luke 9:23).

Worshipping God calls for selflessness. You cannot be selfish while worshipping God. Abel was not thinking of himself when he gave God the sacrifice that was worthy of acceptance. Worshipping God causes you to reflect upon Him, His magnificence, His power and glory. It causes you to reflect upon His goodness. Not only does worship cause us to reflect upon our relationship with God, but it also moves us to look at our relationship with others. God desires for the body of Christ to be unified. The only way this can be achieved is that we move totally and completely out of self.

DISCUSSION QUESTIONS

1) What sacrifices have you made unto the Lord? Was He pleased?

_____

_____

_____

_____

_____

2) In what way do you serve God? Can others see how you are building the kingdom?

_____

_____

_____

_____

_____

3) Is selfishness a part of your character? What areas in your life does God want you to sacrifice for Him?

_____

_____

_____

_____

_____

You Must Have Faith in Your Walk

By faith Enoch was taken away from this life, so that he did not experience death; he could not be found, because God had taken him away. For before he was taken, he was commended as one who pleased God (Hebrews 11:5).

Genesis 5:22 says that Enoch walked with God. The Bible does not record a lot of information about Enoch. He lived 365 years. He was the father of Methusaleh, who lived to be 969. The great thing known about Enoch, which was important enough to repeat, was that Enoch walked with God. He was so dedicated and devoted to God that he did not die. So much so that he did not die. The Bible says he was "taken away" from earth to heaven (Hebrews 11:5). That might sound scary, but we all must go sometime; why not skip death and go directly to the Father? Enoch was the only individual who received this honor. Enoch's example of walking with God reveals that you must desire the savior, denounce sin, and deny self.

Desire the Savior

Having faith in your walk requires you to desire to walk with God. As you walk with God, you will hunger and thirst after Him. Your relationship with Him moves from the superficial level to a deep level of commitment and obedience. Your desire for Him moves from only wanting Him for crisis intervention, to yearning for a daily walk with Him. Walking with God means to have faith in Him over the long haul. It means trusting Him when you cannot trace Him. When you desire the Savior you will spend time with Him. You will be satisfied by being in His presence. Your relationship will not be about what God can give and provide for you, but what you can give to Him.

Denounce Sin

Walking with God causes you to deal with unconfessed sin in your life. It is impossible to walk in faith and walk in sin at the same time. Satan will try to make you think you can, but you can't. Sin interferes with your *fellowship* with God. Please understand that I did not say it interferes with your *relationship* with God. Once you have accepted Christ, nothing can take away your salvation. That Father/child relationship can never be severed. However, your fellowship will be affected when you hold unconfessed sin in your heart (Psalm 66:18). The good news is that God promises to forgive and cleanse you when you confess your sins to Him (1 John 1:9). Don't allow Satan to make you become desensitized to the working of sin in your life. Don't allow anything to give him a foothold to enter into your life to make strongholds. Confess your sins daily.

Deny Self

Walking with God requires you to deny yourself. Matthew 16:24 says, "If anyone would come after me, he must deny himself and take up his cross and follow me." I have learned this is a growing process. Many times this is what non-Christians and new Christians fear. They feel once they accept Christ they have to give up everything that once brought them happiness. Rest assured, God understands that denying self is a gradual process. Yes, there may be some things in your life for which God will give immediate conviction. Not only will He put the desire in your heart to give it up, but He will also empower you through the Holy Spirit to give it up. It will become your desire to give it up because once you are in Christ, you become a new creature (2 Corinthians 5:17). Over time, God will show you other areas in your life that need to be purged. It may be a habit, a desire, a friend, associates, your job, your expectations, pride, unforgiveness, and the list goes on. Many times the things God commands you to deny are the things that mean the most to you. He wants you to seek Him first (Matthew 6:33). Know that if God shows you something you need to deny for Him, it is because He has something far greater He wants to give you in exchange. Ultimately, He is trying to shape your life so that it will reflect more of Him and less of you.

DISCUSSION QUESTIONS

1) Can it be said that you walk with God? Do you allow Him to govern your actions, thoughts and decisions—even when times are difficult?

_____

_____

_____

_____

_____

2) Is there any unconfessed sin in your life? Why? How is it affecting your walk with God?

_____

_____

_____

_____

_____

3) Are there things or situations in your life that are getting in the way of your relationship with God? What is it? Why haven't you let it go?

_____

_____

_____

_____

_____

YOU MUST HAVE FAITH IN YOUR WORK

By faith Noah, when warned about things not yet seen, in holy fear built an ark to save his family. By his faith he condemned the world and became heir of the righteousness that comes by faith (Hebrews 11:7).

Many believers are familiar with the story of Noah, found in Genesis 6. Noah was obedient to God and built an ark when the people around him probably thought he was crazy. He kept telling the people that God said it was going to rain, but they didn't believe him. They laughed at him. They ignored his warnings, but Noah kept working. Noah's faith teaches us to obey the omnipotent one, overlook the obvious, and overcome the obstacles.

Obey the Omnipotent One

The journey of faith requires you to obey God. It is one thing to read the Word, hear the Word, teach the Word, and have knowledge of the Word, however, you must take it one step further: obey the Word. God is calling for obedience. He wants you to take Him at His Word and trust Him in everything. Faith requires obedience. You cannot have faith without being obedient and you cannot be obedient without having faith. Like Noah, you may not always have the total picture when God tells you to do something, but you must trust God enough to know that He works all things out for your good (Romans 8:28). Isaiah 1:19 says that you must be willing and obedient to eat the good of the land. God blesses those who are willing and obedient.

Overlook the Obvious

You must understand that the Christian walk involves another realm outside of what you can see. God is all-powerful and all-knowing. He operates far beyond what you are able to see, feel, or even comprehend. You must always be in tune with God through the Word, praying and fasting, because this is what sharpens your spiritual vision. Isaiah 55:8 says, "For my thoughts are not your thoughts, neither are your ways my ways." You will never be able to figure God out, but as you have faith in your work, God gives you spiritual insight, leads, guides and directs you.

Overcome the Obstacles

I'm sure Noah had to overcome many obstacles as he worked to build the ark God had commanded him to build. As previously stated, many probably talked about him, criticized and ridiculed him. Perhaps his family did not understand and many questioned his actions. But Noah kept right on building. Just as Noah did, you too must overcome the obstacles as you work for God. Others may not understand. They may talk about you and even laugh at you. They may ask, "Why are you doing that?" But you must heed the Word of God. For you know He is the author and finisher of your faith (Hebrews 12:2) and He rewards those who diligently seek Him (Hebrews 11:6).

DISCUSSION QUESTIONS

1) Has God ever told you to do something that you didn't understand? What did you do?

_____

_____

_____

_____

_____

2) Has God given you a vision that may seem impossible? What is it? If you shared it with others, how did they respond?

_____

_____

_____

_____

_____

3) What obstacles have you encountered as you sought to work for God? How did you handle them?

_____

_____

_____

_____

As you walk the journey of faith, you must live life with the anticipation of what is ahead rather than the frustration of what is behind. Paul said, "Brothers, I do not consider myself yet to have taken hold of it. But one thing I do: Forgetting what is behind and straining toward what is ahead, I press on toward the goal to win the prize for which God has called me heavenward in Christ Jesus" (Philippians 3:13–14). You must live life with the anticipation of what God has promised rather than the frustration of your present circumstances. You must trust God. Romans 8:24–25 says, "For in this hope we were saved. But hope that is seen is no hope at all. Who hopes for what he already has? But if we hope for what we do not yet have, we wait for it patiently." In other words, you can have faith even though you may not see victory with the physical eye; God has given you victory in your spiritual vision and you must wait with patience for it to come to pass. Hallelujah!

LESSON 3 – THE JOURNEY OF FAITH

Goal: To put your faith to work

Homework Assignment:

- Commit to trust God in an area of your life in which you have lacked faith.

- Write in your journal, an area in your life in which you have struggled because of lack of faith. Find scriptures that can give you strength in those areas of your life. Make a commitment to study, memorize, and obey these scriptures.

- Record in your journal what God does because of you putting your faith into action.

_____

_____

_____

Becoming a Woman of Prayer

Peter was therefore kept in prison, but prayer was made without ceasing of the church unto God for him (Acts 12:5 KJV).

What Is Prayer?

When I was a new convert, I recalled hearing the "seasoned saints" of the church pray during Sunday morning worship and at midweek prayer meeting. They prayed strong, bold prayers and I longed to pray like them. Not only did I not know how to pray, but also I was afraid to pray, especially publicly. In my consuming desire to learn how to pray, I wrote a letter to my spiritual mother, Mrs. Ethel Mars in Chicago, Illinois. I told her of my yearning to learn how to pray. I expected her to respond with a five-page list of things I had to do. Instead, her response was very simple. She wrote and said, "Wanda, you have already made the first step. God has put the desire in your heart to pray. Because of that your prayer life will increase as you grow spiritually. Don't push. It will come. It is a growing process. Just grow slow and natural." She encouraged me to continue to go to mid-week prayer meetings even though I was afraid to pray aloud. She was right, the day finally came when I gained enough courage to lead the prayer. It wasn't a seasoned, strong, bold prayer like the others, but it was a sincere prayer. Mrs. Mars may not have given me step-by-step instructions on how to pray, but she said enough to let a fifteen-year-old new Christian know that prayer was essential to the life of the believer and that as I grew in Christ so would my prayer life.

Prayer is intimate communication with God. It is the sharing of your heart and the seeking of God's heart. Prayer is a child reaching out to the Father. It is the Father affirming His child. Prayer allows God in the secret places of your life. It is talking and listening to God. In his book, *Celebration of Discipline*, Richard Foster writes:

Prayer catapults us onto the frontier of the spiritual life. Of all the Spiritual Disciplines, prayer is the most central because it ushers us into perpetual communion with the Father. Meditation introduces us to the inner life, fasting is an accompanying means, study transforms our minds, but it is the Discipline of prayer that brings us into the deepest and highest work of the human spirit. Real prayer is life creating and life changing.

Prayer is essential to every believer. This lesson will address five questions: (1) Why should you pray? (2) How should you pray? (3) How does prayer work? (4) What are some hindrances of prayer? And (5) What are the results of prayer?

WHY SHOULD YOU PRAY?

The answer to this question is easy. We should pray because as children of God, we are commanded to pray. Matthew 26:41 says to ". . . watch and pray so that you will not fall into temptation. The spirit is willing, but the body is weak." Luke 18:1 says men should always pray and not faint. Ephesians 6:18 tells us, we should pray always with prayer and supplication in the Spirit. First Thessalonians 5:17 admonishes us to "pray continually." God's Word clearly instructs us to pray. The question may be asked, "Why does God instruct us to pray when He is omnipresent (everywhere), omnipotent (all-powerful) and omniscient (all-knowing)?" or, "Why should we pray when God is everywhere, in control of all things and knows everything?" The answer is, God has chosen the vehicle of prayer to accomplish His work in the lives of His children. We must understand that because God's ways are not our ways and His thoughts are not our thoughts (Isaiah 55:8), we will never fully understand or ever figure God out. Because of our faith and belief in God, there are many things about the Christian walk we must accept at face value. Paul said it best, "Now we see but a poor reflection as in a mirror; then we shall see face to face. Now I know in part; then I shall know fully, even as I am fully known" (1 Corinthians 13:12). In other words, Paul was saying, we do not understand everything now, but one day we will. The command to pray is one of those things. We pray because God commands us to pray and God works in the lives of His people through prayer. Even though we do not fully understand how or why this is so, believe me, we will understand it better by and by!

God used prayer in biblical times to transform people and change circumstances. Moses prayed and God provided water for the children of Israel (Exodus 15:24–25). Hannah prayed and God blessed her with a child (1 Samuel 1:27). Jehoshaphat prayed and God delivered him and the people of Judah out of the hands of their enemies (2 Chronicles 18–20). Ezra prayed and God entreated him (Ezra 8:23). Samuel prayed for Israel and they were victorious over the Philistines (1 Samuel 7:10). The early church prayed and they were all filled with the Holy Ghost (Acts 4:31). Even the disciples recognized the significance of prayer. One of them went to Jesus in Luke 11:1 and asked Him to teach them to pray. Most importantly, Jesus Himself prayed. Since Jesus saw the need to pray, how much more should we pray?

DISCUSSION QUESTIONS

1) Do you sometimes find it difficult to pray? Why or why not?

_____

_____

_____

_____

_____

2) If you don't feel like praying, will your prayer be sincere?

_____

_____

_____

_____

_____

3) What can you do to become more consistent in your prayer life?

_____

_____

_____

_____

_____

How Should You Pray?

Although there is no prescribed prayer, Jesus provided what David Jeremiah called a roadmap for prayer with principles, that when followed, provide tools for an effective prayer life for the believer. As you examine the model prayer (the Lord's Prayer) taught by Jesus Himself in Luke 11 (KJV), there are various principles that are noteworthy.

Praise

"Our Father, who art in heaven, hollowed be thy name." Our prayers should begin with praise and adoration to God. When we omit praise, our prayers become nothing but a wish list presented to God for His granting. There are times when I come home after being gone to a conference for a couple of days and my children, who are various ages with different needs, all greet me with their agendas and concerns. No one says, "Hello, Mom, we missed you, we're glad you're home." Their only acknowledgement of my presence is their list of requests. I usually stop them and say, "Can I at least get a hug or a welcome home Mom"? Likewise, we must also take note of the way we approach God in prayer. Do we go to Him with a "laundry list" of "I need . . ." and "I want . . ." or do we greet Him with praise and adoration? God desires us to praise Him with the fruit of our lips (Hebrews 13:15). We must bless the Lord at all times. His praise should continually be in our mouths (Psalms 34:1).

Priorities

"Thy kingdom come thy will be done on earth as it is in heaven." Prayer is not getting our will done in heaven, but it is getting God's will done on earth. God promises to answer our prayers when we pray according to His will (1 John 5:14). When our priorities are according to God's will, they will line up with the Word of God.

Provision

"Give us this day our daily bread." We must trust God to provide for our needs. God promises to provide our physical bread (Matthew 6:25) and He will also provide our spiritual food (Matthew 4:4, Luke 4:4). It is important to remember that we must seek God to be fed. He feeds those who are hungry and desire the sincere milk of the Word (1 Peter 2:2). However, we can only be fed when we come to the table. In other words, we can only receive spiritual nourishment when we feast on the Word of God.

Personal Relationship

"Forgive us our debts as we forgive our debtors." The cross of Calvary does not only extend vertically, but it also extends horizontally. Christianity does not only deal with how we relate to God, but it also deals with how we relate to one another. God is just as concerned about our relationships with others as He is with our relationship with Him. Therefore, just as we pray and ask God to forgive us of our sins, we should also forgive those who have offended us.

Protection

"Lead us not into temptation, but deliver us from evil." The life of the believer involves constant spiritual warfare. We do not war in the flesh, our weapons are mighty through God (2 Corinthians 10:3–4) who protects us and fights the battle for us. Satan, our enemy, is always at work seeking to discourage and deter us, but thanks be to God, we are victorious through Christ Jesus. John 10:10 says, Satan came to kill, steal, and destroy, but Jesus came that we might have life and that we might have it more abundantly.

Promise

"For thine is the kingdom and the power and the glory forever. Amen." As a child of God, we have the promise that God is sovereign. He reigns forevermore. No matter what we may be going through or how bleak our circumstances may appear, God is in control. At His name every knee shall bow and every tongue shall confess that Jesus is Lord (Philippians 2:11). That's good news.

Jesus provided this prayer as a model to help believers gain the principles in praying effectively. Another common way to remember the components of prayer is through the acronym ACTSIL.

1) ADORATION—praise and worship to God

2) CONFESSION—confession of sins

3) THANKSGIVING—thanking God for His many blessings

4) SUPPLICATION—making requests for yourself

5) INTERCESSORY—making requests for others

6) LISTENING—taking time to hear from God

Acts 12:5 provides another model for prayer. There, we find King Herod, who was seeking to persecute the church, had thrown Peter in jail. King Herod had previously killed James, the brother of John and now had Peter arrested with the intention of killing him. When the church heard the news, they gathered for prayer. The verse says, "Peter was therefore kept in prison, but prayer was made without ceasing of the church unto God for him" (Acts 12:5 KJV). There are some principles for prayer in this verse.

Petition

". . . prayer was made . . ." When the church heard that Peter was in prison, they petitioned God in prayer. The Bible says *prayer was made*. As children of God, we have the awesome privilege of petitioning God for ourselves and others. Philippians 4:6 says, "Do not be anxious about anything, but in everything, by prayer and petition, with thanksgiving, present your requests to God." Isn't it a blessing to know we can talk to God about everything? We serve a God who can be touched by our pain and infirmities (Hebrews 4:15). Yes, we serve a God who understands whatever we may be going through. The Word also says that we can go boldly before the throne and obtain mercy, and find grace to help in the time of need (Hebrews 4:16). We can cast our cares upon Him because He cares for us (1 Peter 5:7).

Persistence

". . . without ceasing . . ." The Bible says they prayed without ceasing. In other words, they were persistent in their praying. Often, when the results you desire are not seen, the temptation is to give up. However, you must remain steadfast, unmovable, always abounding in the work of the Lord, for your labor is not in vain (1 Corinthians 15:58). When you want something bad enough, you keep at it until it has been accomplished; so it is with your prayers—you must persistently pray. God wants to know just how much you desire what you are praying for. Do you desire it enough to remain faithful? Do you desire it enough to be obedient? Are you willing to endure the hardships or will you give up when the going gets tough? You must remember that persistence in prayer is for your benefit, not God's.

Public

The Scripture says that prayer was made, without ceasing, *of the church*. Their prayers were public; they joined together and prayed as the body of Christ. This shows the importance of the body of believers coming together to touch and agree through prayer. The Bible says where two or three are gathered together in God's name, He will be in the midst (Matthew 18:20). Therefore, you know that God is present during corporate prayer. Even Jesus saw the need to come together with others to pray (Matthew 11, Luke 3, John 11, John 17). You can touch and agree in faith with other believers and do mighty things in the name of Jesus (Matthew 18:19). The more people who are praying for something, the more voices are being lifted to heaven. When your prayers are according to the will of God, He will move because He is faithful to His Word. God is not a man that He should lie (Numbers 23:19).

Personal

The prayer was personal because it was, as the text says, *unto God*. As a believer, you have direct access to your Savior. You do not have to ask the priest to pray on your behalf. You can pray to the Father for yourself. God's Word says that you can go boldly to the throne of God (Hebrews 4:16). I remember when our son, Dwight, was about six years old, he had a friend over to play. After being outside playing for a while, the two boys were hot and tired. Dwight had a bright idea. He knew there were Popsicles in the refrigerator. Dwight sent his friend to ask his (Dwight's) dad if they could have a

Popsicle. "Mr. Davis, Dwight told me to ask you if we could have a Popsicle." "Where is Dwight?" his dad questioned. "Tell him I said come here." When Dwight came, his dad explained to him, "Son, I am *your* father. You do not have to send your friend to ask me for something you want. Nor do you have to be afraid to come ask yourself. Because I am your father, you can come to me at anytime about anything." This is the same message God has for us. We are His children and we can make our prayers personal. In addition, God is concerned about every detail of our life. Nothing is too small. We can talk to Him for ourselves. Praise the Lord!

Proxy

The church was praying for Peter. The Scripture says prayer was made without ceasing, of the church, *for him.* The church was praying on Peter's behalf. Although our prayers can be personal, there are times when we desire or perhaps need the prayers of others. The word *proxy* means an authorized agent or substitute; one deputized to act for another. Jesus stands in proxy for us as He mediates between the Father and us, presenting us as righteous. As we pray proxy prayers, we are not presenting others as righteous or reconciling them to God, Jesus has already done that, but we are praying for their particular situation and for the release of God's power in their lives.

DISCUSSION QUESTIONS

1) What is the Lord's Prayer?

_____

_____

_____

_____

_____

2) How should the Lord's model prayer affect your personal prayers?

_____

_____

_____

_____

_____

3) What does the acronym ACTSIL stand for? How might this be helpful when you pray?

A _____

C _____

T _____

S _____

I _____

L _____

_____

_____

_____

_____

How Does Prayer Work?

Now that you have established what prayer is and why and how you should pray, you may ask the question, "How does prayer work?" The first thing you must understand is that although God is all-powerful and all-knowing, He still desires your prayers. He has established prayer as the means by which He works in the lives of people. Ezekiel 22:30–31 reveals the importance of prayer and how it works.

> I looked for a man among them who would build up the wall and stand before me in the gap on behalf of the land so I would not have to destroy it, but I found none. So I will pour out my wrath on them and consume them with my fiery anger, bringing down on their heads all they have done, declares the Sovereign Lord.

The Jews had been disobedient and God poured out His wrath upon them. However, if there had been just one person to pray on their behalf, God would have spared them. God's word is clearly saying, He looked for someone to intercede on the behalf of the people. If there had just been one, He would have shown mercy. But, because He found no one, He poured out His wrath upon them. How many times has God searched for just one person to pray for a situation and He found no one? Are you guilty of not praying for someone or for some situation? Your prayer could be the one that changes things.

The Word of God says, "I tell you the truth, whatever you bind on earth will be bound in heaven, and whatever you loose on earth will be loosed in heaven" (Matthew 18:18). This lets us know that through Christ, we have the power to shake up some things on earth. Our divine connection must be used in the *right* way. Now the big question is, "What is the right way?" The answer is simple: according to God's will. God answers prayer in one of three ways—yes, no or wait. If you want to receive fewer "No's," you must learn to pray according to God's will. God's Word says, "This is the confidence we have in approaching God: that if we ask anything according to his will, he hears us. And if we know that he hears us—whatever we ask—we know that we have what we asked of him" (1 John 5:14–15). Praying according to God's will simply means praying that which is in accordance with God's Word. The test to determine if what you are praying for is in accordance with God's Word is to find a Scripture that supports what you are praying about. If it isn't in the Word of God, more than likely it is not according to His will. Equally important as praying in line with God's Word is praying with the right motivations. A young lady shared with me how she had been praying for years for her marriage. She was asking God for a marriage with more emotional intimacy. She desired more time, attention, and affection from her spouse. As we talked, God began to reveal that on the surface, her prayers were according to God's will. It is certainly God's will for a husband and wife to share emotional intimacy and have a close relationship. The Bible says a husband shall leave his father and mother and cleave to his wife. It says the two shall become one (Genesis 2:24). The husband is to rejoice with the wife of his youth (Proverbs 5:18). Certainly her prayers were in line with the Word of God.

However, as we continued to talk, red flags began to surface. Although her prayer was in agreement with the Word of God, the motivation for her prayer was not. The Bible says, "When you ask, you do not receive, because you ask with wrong motives, that you may spend what you get on your pleasures" (James 4:3). In other words, sometimes God says no, because your intentions and motivations are not right. This woman was praying this prayer because of her own needs and desires that longed to be met by her husband. If God had granted that prayer, she may have been overtaken by the attention and affection from her husband and probably would have forgotten about God. It was not until she gained that same appetite for a relationship with God that she had for her husband that God gave her that emotional intimacy. By that time, her prayer had changed. She was no longer asking God for her husband to have a more intimate relationship with her, but she was praying, "Lord, let my husband have a more intimate relationship with You." She had learned through her own walk with the Lord that if her husband had a stronger relationship with God, he would then love her even more. This same lady now shares her testimony of how God worked in their marriage and brought them closer together.

You must understand that prayer is not getting your will done in heaven, but it is getting God's will done on earth. When you pray, you open the door for God's will to be manifested in your situation. You must keep the channels of prayer clear with God by praying according to His Word and praying with the right motivation. The only motivation for your prayers should be that God would receive glory. Ask yourself, "Will God receive glory from what I am praying for?" God received the glory once my friend changed her prayer. How about you? Do you need to change what you've been praying about?

Fasting as you pray also opens the channels between you and God. Fasting involves abstaining from food or other things for a specified amount of time for a spiritual purpose. We will deal with fasting in detail in Lesson 7.

DISCUSSION QUESTIONS

1) How does prayer work?

_____

_____

_____

_____

_____

2) If God is all-knowing and He already knows my situation, why do I need to pray?

_____

_____

_____

_____

_____

3) Why is the motivation for prayer just as important as the subject of prayer?

_____

_____

_____

_____

_____

4) Based on what you have just learned in this lesson, is there a prayer you have been praying that you could change to align more with God's will? If so, how should it be changed?

_____

_____

_____

_____

_____

WHAT ARE SOME HINDRANCES OF PRAYER?

If you are concerned about having an effective prayer life, you will want to be aware of those things that hinder your prayers. The Bible gives clear insight in this area.

DISOBEDIENCE—Deuteronomy 1:45; 1 Samuel 14:37; 28:6

Although God is loving and forgiving, when you are disobedient, sometimes there are grave consequences.

PRIVATE SIN—Psalms 66:18

Man may not see your sins, but God knows the heart. Secret sin will hinder your prayers.

INDIFFERENCE—Proverbs 1:28

Take heed not to reject the wisdom of God. Take caution in becoming self-sufficient.

NEGLIGENCE—Proverbs 21:13

You must be careful not to be like the priest and Levite who passed and left the stranger on the road to Jericho. Choose to be like the Good Samaritan who gave of himself and took the time to care for his brother.

HYPOCRISY—Isaiah 1:15

To do what God commands is not enough. Your heart must be sincere and your motives must be genuine.

INIQUITY—Isaiah 59:2

Unconfessed sin in your life causes God to turn a deaf ear to your prayers.

STUBBORNNESS—Zechariah 7:13

There comes a time when God allows man to suffer the consequences of his sin. If man will not listen to God, God will not listen to man.

DOUBT AND INSTABILITY—James 1:6–8

When you pray to God, you must have faith in Him. You must believe that He can do all things. Doubt causes you to be unstable.

SELFISH MOTIVATIONS—James 4:3

Why you pray is just as important as *what* you pray. God is concerned with your heart and the motivations for your prayers. If you are praying for selfish reasons your prayers will be hindered.

DISCUSSION QUESTION

1) Examine your life. Is there anything that may be hindering your prayers? If so, what is it? What can you do to eliminate it?

_____

_____

_____

_____

_____

_____

_____

_____

_____

_____

_____

_____

WHAT ARE THE RESULTS OF PRAYER?

Prayer brings about results and results bring about more prayer. The more you pray, the more you will see God working in your life. The more you see God working in your life, the more you will want to pray. It has been said that prayer is the key to heaven. When God's children call on Him, He will answer. "Come near to God and he will come near to you. Wash your hands, you sinners, and purify your hearts, you double-minded" (James 4:8). There are three major things that occur when you pray: communion, comfort, and change.

Communion

The primary result of prayer is communion with God. It is through prayer that you gain an intimate relationship with God, where you speak to Him and He speaks to you. Prayer brings you to a position of awareness of God's presence in your life. It is through prayer that you truly experience God in His fullness. Tommy Tenney, author of *God Chasers*, tells the story of coming home after being away for a few days, to find his daughter on the floor playing with her dolls. "Aren't you going to give Daddy a hug?" he asked. His daughter continued to play with the dolls, making it known she really didn't want to stop playing to give her daddy a hug. Finally, she reluctantly went over and gave him a quick hug and went back to the dolls. Tommy was disappointed. He wanted his daughter to run into his arms the minute he stepped into the room. Tommy likens this story to our response to God. God's capacity to receive love from us is greater than our capacity to give. He desires for us to run to Him, to yearn to spend time with Him. However, we are busy with the things of life. We are busy playing with the gifts God has given us; we have forgotten the Giver. We must seek the Giver, not the gifts. Prayer seeks the Giver. Through prayers we go to God. We meet Him in a special place, a place where He stands ready and willing to receive us and meet our needs. It is through prayer that we gain a closer walk with God. We get to know Him rather than know about Him.

Comfort

Prayer brings comfort. As you pray, God speaks His Word into your spirit. It is not by chance, coincidence, or accident that God's Word is coming to you. It is the Holy Spirit speaking to you. When you have prayed according to the will of God, He begins to speak to you with His Word regarding the situation. You can then find peace. God's Word will bring comfort. This is how you have peace in the midst of the storm. Yes, this is where faith steps in because the true test of faith is peace. This may also be a time when you must wait on God. You can have comfort because you know God's Word is true. You know He is faithful. You can be assured that all things will work out for your good (Romans 8:28).

Change

The third result of prayer is change. Maybe you have heard the saying, "Prayer changes things." I can attest that this old saying is true and real. Prayer does change things. Not only does it change things, but it also changes people, situations, circumstances, finances, and families. The list can go on forever. The key to experiencing this change is releasing whatever you are praying about to God. When you release your concerns to God, it allows God's hand to work. You must understand the change you desire may or may not occur. Sometimes God surprises you and you realize that it is not your situation or the other person that needs to change. It may be you who needs changing! This is why releasing the situation to God is so important. As long as you are trying to fix it, change it, maneuver it, or manipulate it, God cannot and will not transform it. You must sit back and allow God to work everything out. A story was told of a little boy who had a broken toy. He tried relentlessly to fix the toy, but to no avail. After trying for hours, he finally gave up and took it to his father to repair it. To his dismay, his dad repaired the toy in a matter of seconds. The child was amazed. His father looked at him and said, "Son, I could have fixed the toy a long time ago, but you wouldn't give it to me." God is looking from on high, watching you struggle with situations. He is standing by ready and able to change them, but you won't give them to Him. Change comes only when you trust God enough to let go and let Him handle the situation.

DISCUSSION QUESTIONS

1) Think of a specific situation where God worked in your life as a result of prayer. How was your life changed?

   _____

   _____

   _____

   _____

   _____

2) Have you experienced communion, comfort, or change in your life as a result of prayer? Explain.

   _____

   _____

   _____

   _____

   _____

God wants all believers to be prayer warriors. He has chosen the vehicle of prayer through which He works in your life as well as others whose lives we impact and influence. I'd like to share with you an entry from my journal written after God spoke to my heart regarding prayer. "Prayer is not getting God to give us what we want—but its ultimate goal and objective is an intimate, personal relationship with God. If what we want happens in the process, then great! If it does not, that's okay too. More than anything, we should allow God to work on the inside of us through our prayers, rather than try to force God to change the outside condition or situation. As we pray, God reveals His will to us. He gives us spiritual vision in the situation; it is this vision that gives us the faith and patience to wait and hold on for God to come through. Sadly, many people never get to this point because they can't move from praying, trying to get God to do what they want Him to do. Therefore, they live in frustration, anxiety, and have no peace. But you can have peace when you know you are walking in God's will! Praise the Lord!" I challenge you to PUSH in your prayers: PRAY UNTIL SOMETHING HAPPENS. *Don't be surprised if what happens is a change on the inside of you.*

LESSON 4 – BECOMING A WOMAN OF PRAYER

Goal: To develop an effective prayer life and seek to be intentional in praying

Homework Assignment:

- At the beginning of each week, make a list of things and/or people which you will commit to prayer for that week.

- Designate a specific and consistent time for prayer (i.e. every morning at 5:00 a.m., every evening at 6:30).

- Spend time listening to God.

- Journal how God answers your prayers and what He speaks to you.

- Plan to share with the group next time.

Example:

List of Prayer Concerns:
- Mother's illness
- Bob lost his job
- Tommy's salvation
- Safety for my children
- World peace
- Improvement of my neighborhood
- James and Tina's marriage
- My pastor and his family
- Personal concerns

Prayer Schedule:

Monday

- Mother's illness and for the healing (physical and spiritual) of all who are sick
- Bob's job loss and for all who are unemployed and having financial problems

Tuesday

- Tommy's salvation and for all who do not know the Lord as their personal Savior
- Safety for my children and for the safety of all children
- World peace for the nation and for our national leaders and armed forces

Wednesday (and so on for each day of the week)

- Improvement of my neighborhood and for all neighborhoods
- James and Tina's marriage and for all marriages
- For my pastor and his family; for all clergy families and the universal body of Christ
- My personal concerns

_____

_____

_____

_____

_____

_____

_____

_____

_____

_____

_____

_____

_____

_____

_____

_____

How to Fight the Battle and Win: Understanding Spiritual Warfare

Put on the full armor of God so that you can take your stand against the devil's schemes. For our struggle is not against flesh and blood, but against the rulers, against the authorities, against the powers of this dark world and against the spiritual forces of evil in the heavenly realms (Ephesians 6:11–12).

When you and I accepted Christ as our personal Savior, we enlisted in the greatest war in the history of mankind—spiritual warfare. Each day we face it. It cannot be prevented or avoided. We can never become immune to it or exempt from it. Spiritual warfare is real and as Christians, we cannot ignore it or pretend it does not exist. H. Beecher Hicks, Jr. says in his book, *Preaching Through a Storm* that we are all in one of three places as it relates to the storms of life. We are either in a storm, just coming out of a storm, or headed toward a storm. The reality of spiritual warfare may sound discouraging, but it doesn't have to because every believer is victorious through Christ Jesus. By the power of the blood of Jesus, every child of God is an overcomer. Satan is defeated. Hallelujah, that's good news! It is because of our knowledge of who we are in Christ (Lesson 1) that we know we have a blessed hope through Jesus Christ. Because of this hope, we can face whatever the devil may try to throw our way.

Spiritual warfare is defined by Tony Evans as "that conflict being waged in the invisible, spiritual realm that is being manifest in the visible, physical realm" (Evans, p. 19). You might say it is a war in the heavenlies between God and Satan with man caught in the crossfire. John 10:10a says the thief comes to steal, kill and destroy. He knows he cannot take away your salvation because the Word of God says that no man shall pluck you out of His hand (John 10:29); therefore Satan does whatever he can to prevent you from staying focused on your eternal goal.

It is Satan's goal to distract and discourage God's children. By now you are probably asking the big question: "Why?" This is a very good question and an extremely important one. As a Christian, understanding why you are in the battle, will help you be victorious. The battle began with Lucifer's rebellion against God in heaven. Lucifer was one of God's most beautiful angels. Not only was he beautiful, but he could also sing. He walked in God's holy presence. He held the highest position that God could give to one of His creatures. Ezekiel 28:14 refers to him as the "anointed guardian cherub." But all of this went to Lucifer's head and he rebelled against God. So, God threw Lucifer and one third of heaven's angels out of heaven and cast them to the ground (Ezekiel 28:17). Ever since that day, there has been a battle between God and Satan. The earth has become a "holding place" for Satan and his angels (which are often referred to as demons or imps) until their sentence is carried out.

As an act of revenge, Satan works to kill, steal, and destroy that which means most to God, His children. You might say God's children are caught in the crossfire. The real battle is between God and Satan. This is why the Bible says the battle is not yours. It's the Lord's. It also tells you ". . . the weapons we fight with are not the weapons of the world. On the contrary, they have divine power to demolish strongholds. We demolish arguments and every pretension that sets itself up against the knowledge of God, and we take captive every thought to make it obedient to Christ" (2 Corinthians 10:4–5). Though we physically experience the battle on earth, we must remember it is also in the heavenlies. "Our struggle is not against flesh and blood, but against the rulers, against the authorities, against the powers of this dark world and against the spiritual forces of evil in the heavenly realms" (Ephesians 6:12).

Tony Evans, in his book *The Battle is the Lord's*, explains there are two worldviews in life. A person's worldview is the way they perceive reality and determines how they will respond to the attacks of the enemy in their life. There are some individuals who hold a scientific worldview, which is a natural or materialistic worldview. People with this worldview try to answer life's problems in the natural with solutions that are explainable, measurable, physical and visible. Individuals who hold a spiritual worldview understand there is a realm outside of the physical. Because they believe our world is governed by a power and source not of our own, they approach problems differently and seek different solutions. Those with a spiritual worldview understand that their problems are spiritual, and require spiritual solutions.

As a child of God, it is important that you are able to identify the type of battle you face in spiritual warfare. Knowing the type of battle you are in can determine your success or failure in the battle. I have put spiritual battles into three categories, which I will call sovereign storms, satanic storms, and sinful storms. Knowing which storm you face not only helps determine your battle plan, but also lets you know how you should respond and may help you understand what God is trying to accomplish in you through the storm.

SOVEREIGN STORMS

Storms from the Divine

Storms from the Divine are sovereign storms. They are God-sent storms. They do not necessarily come into your life because of anything you have done or not done. They simply come so that God will be glorified. John 9 tells the story of a man who was born blind. The disciples went to Jesus and asked, "Why was this man born blind? Did he sin? Did his parents sin and cause him to be born blind?" In other words, the disciples were asking who was to blame for this terrible thing in this man's life. Was he being punished? Jesus answered them by saying, "Neither this man nor his parents sinned, but this happened so that the work of God might be displayed in his life" (John 9:3). Jesus was saying that this situation had not come to this man because of anything he or his parents did wrong, but it came so God might be glorified. God allows some storms to come in your life so that you will remember to praise, worship, and glorify Him.

SATANIC STORMS

Storms from the Devil

Satanic storms are God allowed. The story of Job is a perfect example of a satanic storm. The Bible describes Job as a perfect, upright man, one who feared God and shunned evil (Job 1:1). He was the greatest of all men in the east. He made sacrifices to the Lord regularly on the behalf of his sons in case they had sinned. One day Satan went before the Lord. The Lord said to Satan, "Where have you come from?" Satan answered the Lord, "From roaming through the earth and going back and forth in it" (Job 1:7). God then asked, "Have you considered my servant Job? There is no one on earth like him" (Job 1:8). Satan then attacked Job and stripped him of everything—his children, cattle and even his health. Through all of this, Job continued to give God praise. Remember, God wants the glory in whatever you go through. The story ends on a high with God restoring to Job twice as much than he had before. You must remember that satanic storms only come when God allows them. When He allows them, He controls them. He will never allow you to go through more than you can handle. The temperature may get extreme, but God always has His hand on the thermostat. Satan's motive in this storm is to destroy you, but God uses this same storm to shape and mold you to reflect more of Him. This is why the Word says, ". . . in all things God works for the good of those who love him, who have been called according to his purpose" (Romans 8:28). God can use what appear to be negative things in your life, to be the best thing that could have ever happened to you.

SINFUL STORMS

Storms of Discipline

Storms of discipline are storms that come as a direct result of sin. There are consequences when we disobey God's Word. Although God is loving and forgiving, He also chastises those He loves (Hebrews 12:6). When Nathan confronted David about his sin, he told him there would be grave consequences for his disobedience. "The sword will never depart from your house," David was told. As a result, David experienced the storms of discipline. The baby he and Bathsheba conceived, died (2 Samuel 12:14–18). There was incest and murder among his children (2 Samuel 13). David's son, Amnon, raped his sister Tamar (2 Samuel 13). Amnon was killed by his brother, Absalom. Absalom later rebelled against his father and formed a conspiracy to steal the heart of Israel (2 Samuel 15). He (Absalom) too was eventually killed (2 Samuel 18).

When God allows storms of discipline to enter our lives, He is trying to bring us to repentance. Because God loves us so much, He will give us many opportunities to turn from our sinful ways before He extends His wrath. His wrath may come in many forms from sickness, loss of job, loss of family, loss of joy, and even death. God wants us to get to a place where we cry out to Him admitting we have sinned against Him. First John 1:9 says, "If we confess our sins, he is faithful and just and will forgive us our sins and purify us from all unrighteousness." Thank God that when we go to Him, He is there willing and waiting to forgive us. David prayed for remission of his sins in Psalm 51. This is what God desires us to do when we encounter storms of discipline.

We have discussed the different types of storms so you will know how to respond to the various storms that come in your life. You must remember, God wants and deserves the glory in everything you go through. In every situation you face, God is in control. Ephesians 6 gives us clear instruction on how to fight the battle and win. Just as a soldier in an army must be equipped, armed, and prepared, you too must be equipped, armed, and prepared to face what Satan throws your way. First Peter 5:8 says, "Be self-controlled and alert. Your enemy the devil, prowls around like a roaring lion looking for someone to devour." As a Christian you must be knowledgeable of Satan's tactics and have a plan for victory.

TEXT

Put on the full armor of God so that you can take your stand against the devil's schemes. For our struggle is not against flesh and blood, but against the rulers, against the authorities, against the powers of this dark world and against the spiritual forces of evil in the heavenly realms (Ephesians 6:11–12).

Paul was writing to the saints at Ephesus because the converted Jews in the early churches had a tendency to exclude others. Because they would separate themselves from the Gentiles, the major theme of the book of Ephesians is unity. Paul opens the book by explaining the divine origin of the church. He explains the plan of salvation and its provisions. He embraces the Gentiles who are now children of God. He removes all barriers between the Jews and Gentiles and unites them as one body in Christ. He prays for their spiritual growth. In chapter 4 he urges them to be consistent in their Christian living. He deals with their home life in chapter 5 and it is in chapter 6 that he reveals to them who their real enemy is. It is extremely important that Christians be able to identify the real enemy. Many times we have what I call, "mislocated battlefields." We fight each other when we should be fighting Satan. It's imperative to remember that we are actually on the same team. There are three things you must know if you want to be successful in the battle: you must know the source of your strength, you must know the strategy of Satan, and you must know the security of the saint.

YOU MUST KNOW THE SOURCE OF YOUR STRENGTH—THE SAVIOR

Ephesians 6:10 says, "Finally, be strong in the Lord and in his mighty power." As a child of God, your only success lies in the fact that you recognize you have one power source: God and God alone. Sometimes the storms of life will take their toll on you and cause you to feel you can't go on, but you must be strong in the Lord and in the power of *His* might, not your own. This means you must respond to trials and tribulations God's way. You should not take matters into your own hands. Why? Because ". . . though we live in the world, we do not wage war as the world does. The weapons we fight with are not the weapons of the world. On the contrary, they have divine power to demolish strongholds. We demolish arguments and every pretension that sets itself up against the knowledge of God, and we take captive every thought to make it obedient to Christ" (2 Corinthians 10:3–5).

You do not have the means, resources, or knowledge to fight the enemy with your own strength. Therefore, you must rely on the Savior. Relying on the Savior requires you to take your hands off the situation. This means you must release the situation to God. Many times our trials are intensified and lengthened because of our disobedience and determination to handle it. I once heard a preacher say, "God will keep you in the classroom until you pass the test." Many times you stand in the way of your victory. God becomes the source of your strength as you yield to Him.

In 2 Chronicles 20, Jehosaphat heard the news of the children of Moab, Ammon and the Ammonites, coming against him. The Bible says he sought the Lord, proclaimed a fast, prayed and began to reflect upon the goodness of God and His previous blessings to them. This is how you allow God to be your strength.

SEEK THE LORD

Study God's Word. Allow it to dwell richly in you. Study it consistently, for it is your spiritual nourishment and without it you will be weak, malnourished, and defeated. Not only must you study God's Word, but in your trials you must also obey His Word. You are most vulnerable to giving in to Satan when you are going through difficult times in your life. It is important to seek to be obedient to what God would have you do. It does not matter what you may face or who may have hurt you; God is holding you accountable for your response. Psalm 18:20 says, "The Lord has dealt with me according to my righteousness; according to the cleanness of my hands he has rewarded me." You have a responsibility as a child of God, to walk upright. My motto is "do the right thing."

FAST

We will study about fasting in lesson 7, but fasting is a strong weapon in spiritual warfare. It alarms God of a 911 situation when you sacrifice for a spiritual purpose. God honors your sacrifice. He hears your cries and He responds in love.

PRAYER

Prayer is the way you connect with God. Not only do you talk with Him, but He also speaks to you. The Word says you are to pray without ceasing (1 Thessalonians 5:17). When you face spiritual battles, your solution and victory lies in telling God—not others.

REFLECTION

Jehosaphat began to reflect upon their previous deliverance. Through your trials it is good to reflect upon God's goodness and your previous triumphs. Remembering God's faithfulness in your past experiences will strengthen your faith in the present.

DISCUSSION QUESTIONS

1) Can you identify some storms in your life and categorize them as sovereign, satanic, or sinful? What do you feel God was trying to accomplish through these storms?

_____

_____

_____

_____

2) How have you handled storms in your life? Did you release them to God or did you attempt to take matters into your own hands?

_____

_____

_____

_____

3) Considering how you handled the storms in your life, what was the outcome?

_____

_____

_____

_____

4) How can you allow God to be the source of your strength?

_____

_____

_____

_____

You Must Know the Strategy of Satan—Spiritual Warfare

For our struggle is not against flesh and blood, but against the rulers, against the authorities, against the powers of this dark world and against the spiritual forces of evil in the heavenly realms (Ephesians 6:12).

You must remember that no matter how things may appear, the battle you are engaged in is not against flesh and blood. It is not a battle you can see with the physical eye. You cannot look your enemy in the eye. Therefore, the person or people you believe to be your enemy is not your real enemy. Your real enemy is Satan and the real battle is in the heavenlies, the invisible realm. This is why human efforts cannot be used to fight the battle. Every Christian needs to understand the strategy of Satan.

When I was in high school I had a friend who played on the varsity basketball team. He told me that during practice his team would watch videos of their opponent's team. They would spend hours reviewing the tape to study the strategy of the opposing team. After studying the tapes, it was imperative that they develop a plan of action. As a Christian you must study your opponent, Satan. You must have knowledge of his schemes, devices, and strategies and you must also have a plan of how you will respond to them. Many times we are defeated in the battle because Satan catches us off guard and we don't know how to respond. As an army soldier goes out with a battle plan of action, equipment and training, you too must be prepared for the battle that is before you.

The Devil's Strategy Has Not Changed

The devil has had the same strategy throughout his existence. Isn't it something to know that he has used the same tactics throughout the years and he's still successful in luring us into his dangerous web? You would think we would eventually catch on. Unfortunately, we still act and react with our flesh and sinful nature, which must be constantly brought under subjection to the authority of Christ Jesus. First John 2:16 describes the three primary areas of temptation: the lust of the eyes, the lust of the flesh, and the pride of life. These are the three areas in which Satan will tempt us. We see this happening at the beginning of time when Satan approached Eve in Genesis 3. As Satan tempted Eve, the Bible says she saw that the tree was good for food. This was lust of the flesh. How many of us today have difficulty denying ourselves of food? This is why fasting is such a challenge. The Bible goes on to say the tree was pleasant to the eyes. This was lust of the eyes. The tree was appealing and beautiful. Satan always dresses sin up and makes it look attractive to the eye. Lastly, we are told the tree was desired to make one wise. This was the pride of life. Eve was made to believe that if she ate of the tree she would become like God. Pride takes you to a point where you begin to trust and believe in self; it defies and disregards God.

We see this same scenario played out in Matthew 4 where Satan appears on the scene again, this time tempting Jesus in the wilderness. Can you identify the three areas of temptation?

1) _____

2) _____

3) _____

Read James 1:13–15. It describes how temptation can lead to sin:

1) Desire—

Verse 14 says, ". . . but each one is tempted when, by his own evil desire . . ." Note that it is your desire and not God's that lead you to sin. Temptation begins with your desire for something or someone. Whenever you have your own agenda you are headed for trouble.

2) Deception—

Verse 14 goes on to say, ". . . he is dragged away and enticed." This is when the devil successfully deceives you. He will dress the sin up to make it look good and enticing, and you find yourself justifying sin. You may find yourself thinking things like, "No one will know . . . Everyone else is doing it . . . It's really not wrong . . . Just this one time won't hurt . . . If it feels good do it . . . God will forgive me . . ." You may even falsely interpret Scripture to justify your desire: "God said He would give me the desires of my heart . . ."

3) Disobedience—

Desire and deception lead to disobedience. James says in verse 15, ". . . after desire has conceived, it gives birth to sin . . ." This is the act of disobedience, where you move from temptation to sin.

4) Death—

Verse 15 goes on to say, ". . . and sin, when it is full-grown, gives birth to death." Sin leads to death. It leads to spiritual death where you become disconnected from God. For a Christian who is saved, it means you are out of fellowship with God. Yes, you will still have a relationship with Him, but there is a barrier between you that prevents you from walking with the Lord the way He desires. You cannot have a clear conscience with God when you are living in sin. A true child of God will have no peace and joy within, when his or her life is not in alignment with the Word of God. Sin can also lead to physical death. Your life can be cut off because of the choice you make to disobey God's Word.

DISCUSSION QUESTIONS

1) Can you identify an area in your life where you are vulnerable to Satan's attack?

_____

_____

_____

_____

_____

2) If you answered the previous question, what is your plan for victory? Pay close attention to the next section in this lesson.

_____

_____

_____

_____

_____

3) Can you see where the four stages of sin have been played out in your life?

_____

_____

_____

_____

_____

You Must Know the Security of the Saint

Put on the full armor of God so that you can take your stand against the devil's schemes. Therefore put on the full armor of God, so that when the day of evil comes, you may be able to stand your ground, and after you have done everything, to stand. Stand firm then, with the belt of truth buckled around your waist, with the breastplate of righteousness in place, and with your feet fitted with the readiness that comes from the gospel of peace. In addition to all this, take up the shield of faith, with which you can extinguish all the flaming arrows of the evil one. Take the helmet of salvation and the sword of the Spirit, which is the word of God (Ephesians 6:11, 13–17).

In Ephesians 6:13–17, Paul gives detailed instructions on the security of God's children. He lets us know what we should wear as armor for protection from the enemy. Without our armor, we are left unprotected, vulnerable and defeated. He likens our spiritual armor to that of the Roman soldiers of that day. Just as they would not go out to war unprotected and girded up, we too should not face the enemy without our suit of armor.

Belt of Truth

The belt was the piece of armor that held everything else together. It is the truth of the Word of God that holds everything else together in your Christian walk. Only the truth of the Word of God can deliver and set you free. The devil is a liar and a deceiver. He works to discourage you by filling the mind with lies. This is why you must take heed to Philippians 4:8 which says, "Finally, brothers, whatever is true, whatever is noble, whatever is right, whatever is pure, whatever is lovely, whatever is admirable—if anything is excellent or praiseworthy—think about such things." Philippians 2:5 also says your attitude should be the same as that of Christ Jesus. Satan works hard at making things appear to be one way when it is truthfully another. You must fill your mind with the Word of God. This is your weapon. Every time Satan puts a negative thought into your mind, you must rebuke it with the truth of God's Word.

Breastplate of Righteousness

The breastplate protected the chest and the heart. The righteousness of Christ is the best protection of the heart during spiritual warfare. Satan has a way of accusing you and making you think you are not what God has made you to be. He may make you doubt your salvation. He may cause you to look at others and believe you are not as holy. Again, these are lies and God's Word is what you must stand on. God declares you righteous, not because of who you are or anything you have done. You are declared righteous because of what Jesus did when He died on the cross for your sins. You became a recipient of His righteousness when you accepted Jesus Christ as your personal Savior.

FEET FITTED WITH READINESS THAT COMES FROM THE GOSPEL OF PEACE

Shoes of brass were worn to protect the soldier's feet as they were prepared to go wherever was necessary to fight the battle. We too should always be prepared to go forth with the gospel of peace. Not only are Christians to share peace, but also we are to live peacefully. Philippians 4:6–7 says, "Do not be anxious about anything, but in everything, by prayer and petition, with thanksgiving, present your requests to God. And the peace of God, which transcends all understanding, will guard your hearts and your minds in Christ Jesus." God will give His children peace as they prepare and engage in battle. Tony Evans, in his book, *The Battle is the Lord's*, explains that as a child of God, you have peace *with* God when you accept Christ as Lord. You have peace *in* God as you grow in Him and face spiritual warfare. You can have this peace because you know that God's Word is true and that He never fails. Whatever you may be going through, God is sovereign and in control. I once heard someone say, "If we serve a God who never sleeps nor slumbers then why should we both stay awake?" You can rest peacefully because you know God will handle all things. First Peter 5:7 says that you can cast your cares upon the Lord for He cares for you. You can have peace in the midst of the storm. Hallelujah!

THE SHIELD OF FAITH

The shield was used for overall protection of the soldier's body. It is the shield of faith that gives the believer overall protection. The shield of faith is believing and acting on the truth, the Word of God. It is one thing for a believer to say he believes in God's Word, but the shield of faith takes that belief one step farther. It causes you to act on the truth you believe. It calls for obedience to the Word of God. A story was once told about a little boy who asked his grandmother the definition of faith. His grandmother replied, "Faith is when God tells me to get up out of this chair and walk through that door, (she points) I get up and walk through that door even though I don't know where God is leading me." The little boy was not satisfied with his grandmother's answer, so he asked a second time, "Grandmother, what is faith?" The grandmother patiently answered the question again, "Son, faith is when God tells me to get up out of this chair and walk through that door (she points again), I get up and walk through that door even though I don't know where God is leading me." By this time the little boy was becoming irritated. He went over to the dresser drawer and pulled out his grandmother's eyeglasses, cleaned them and put them on his grandmother's face. In frustration, he asked his grandmother for the third time. "Grandmother, what is faith?" With all the patience in the world, the grandmother repeated her answer. "Son, I told you. Faith is when God tells me to get up out of this chair and walk through that door (pointing once more), I get up and walk through that door even though I don't know where God is leading me." The little boy was extremely frustrated by now. "Grandmother, look (he points where his grandmother had previously pointed), there is no door there!" The grandmother looked at the little boy and said with confidence, "Faith is when God tells me to get out of this chair and walk through that door (pointing again), I get up and walk through that door even though I don't know where God is leading me. I know there is no door there now, but faith is knowing by the time I get there, a door will be there." Grandmother was letting the boy know that faith is believing God will make a way when there is no way. It is trusting and obeying Him no matter how the circumstances may appear.

THE HELMET OF SALVATION

The helmet was used to protect the soldier's head. The head is vital to the body and without it there can be no life. This is the same with the helmet of salvation for the believer. It is because of Christ Jesus that you have salvation. Your salvation gives you life and makes you victorious in the battle. You are victorious because you are God's child and His Word is full of promises letting you know He will fight your battles for you. He will never leave nor forsake you (Joshua 1:5). He will not put more on you than you can bear. Your salvation entitles you to a comprehensive insurance and assurance policy through Jesus Christ, with full, unlimited coverage.

THE SWORD OF THE SPIRIT

The Sword of the Spirit is the Word of God. The Word of God is your weapon and should be used in spiritual warfare at all times. This is how Jesus defeated Satan in the wilderness (Matthew 4). The Word of God will defeat Satan every time. James 4:7 says, "Submit yourselves, then, to God. Resist the devil, and he will flee from you." Notice the order of the instruction. First, you must submit to God. Submitting to God involves turning to the Word of God, then seeking Him and obeying Him. You must submit to God first to gain the power to resist the devil. After he has been resisted, the Bible says he will flee. God's Word gives strength to His children and puts the devil in his place. Ephesians 6:18 says you should ". . . pray in the Spirit on all occasions with all kinds of prayers and requests. With this in mind, be alert and always keep on praying for all the saints." You must continue in prayer. The Bible says, ". . . whatever you bind on earth will be bound in heaven, and whatever you loose on earth will be loosed in heaven" (Matthew 16:19). Your prayers touch heaven and affect things on earth.

DISCUSSION QUESTIONS

1) Which part of the armor is easiest for you to put on? Explain.

_____

_____

_____

_____

_____

2) Which part of the armor is most difficult for you to put on? Explain.

_____

_____

_____

_____

_____

As a disciple of God, you must know that spiritual Warfare is inevitable. All believers must face it. It will go on until Jesus returns, but you must remember as a child of God that you are victorious. Satan is defeated. No weapon formed against you shall prosper (Isaiah 54:17). Satan has been placed under your feet through Christ Jesus (1 Corinthians 15:25). As a child, I had a toy called Bozo the clown. Bozo was nothing more than a punching bag filled with air. There was a weight in the bottom, which would keep Bozo anchored as I punched him on every side. Every time I hit him, however, he would bounce back up. There was nothing I could do to keep Bozo down. Even if I sat on him, the minute I got up, he would rise again. As a Christian, you are like Bozo the clown. What anchors you is Christ Jesus and you are filled with the Holy Spirit. Every time Satan tries to knock you down you bounce back up. When you put on the whole armor of God, nothing can hold you down.

LESSON 5 – HOW TO FIGHT THE BATTLE AND WIN

Goal: To be able to identify spiritual warfare and experience victory in it

Homework Assignment:

- During times of difficulty, review the lesson and determine what type of warfare you may be experiencing. Pray and ask God what He is seeking to accomplish in your life as a result of what you are going through. Perhaps God is trying to teach you something. What might it be? (To depend on Him and not others; to spend more time with Him; to trust Him more, etc.). God will show you when you ask.

- Similar to Lesson 3, make a list of scriptures that will give you strength during spiritual warfare, memorize and use them when the enemy attacks. Remember the Word of God is your weapon.

- Journal your experience and share with the group next time.

Love that Forgives

But God demonstrates his own love for us in this: While we were still sinners, Christ died for us (Romans 5:8).

As Christians, our desire should be to love as God loves and to forgive as God forgives. However, this may be easier said than done, when we come to realize that sometimes the only way God can teach us certain things is to place challenges pertaining to those things in our lives. He teaches us to trust Him by placing us in situations where we can't rely on ourselves or anyone else. He teaches us patience by putting us in circumstances where we must wait on Him. He teaches us forgiveness by allowing someone to hurt us and He teaches us to love, you guessed it—by planting some "unloving" people in our lives. WOW!

God's Word doesn't beat around the bush when it comes to the subject of love. Your relationship with God is directly related and affected by your relationships with others. I believe God may have stressed love in His Word because He knew we would have a problem with it. First Peter 4:8, 1 John 4:21, 1 Thessalonians 4:9, John 13:35, and John 15:12, are just a few of the many Scriptures in the Bible that tell us to love one another. Christianity is not only how you relate to God, it is also how you relate to others. We talked about faith in Lesson 3. As you study, you will come to realize that love and faith have a lot in common. First, neither of them mean very much until they are put into action. Second, they both must be put into practice in difficult situations. Love, like faith, is an action word. It must be taken off the shelf and used if it is going to be experienced. And yes, it is in those challenging relationships that you find it hard to love. Those are the relationships for which this lesson is written. You don't need a lesson on love to help you love people who are easy to love or for the people in your life who love you. It is those unloving individuals who make it difficult to love, right? You may find after this lesson, that you need a "love makeover."

The goal of this lesson is to help you understand the way God desires for you to love. You must first understand loving God's way has little to do with you. So, move yourself out of the way and prepare to break down the walls of selfishness, pride, unforgiveness and all that ugly stuff that gets in the way of love. God is love. It is not one of the characteristics of His personality, it is who He is. Not only is He love, but also He sets the standard for love. Genuine love is measured by God's love. God has also given us the ultimate example of love. He gave His only Son for us! His son demonstrated love as He walked the earth healing the sick, raising the dead, making the blind see, loving those who cursed Him, doing good to those who hated Him and praying for those who despitefully used and persecuted Him. Even in His dying hour, Jesus prayed, *Father, forgive them, for they do not know what they are doing* (Luke 23:34). THAT'S LOVE!

THE WORLD'S WAY OF LOVING

The world has a set of beliefs about love which conflict with the Word of God. The world says, "If you love me, then I will love you." The worldly steps to love are **a desire**, **decision**, and **demonstration**. First, there is a *desire* or feeling, which usually comes from physical attraction. You meet someone and you feel something. You like what you see and feel so you move to the second step and make the *decision* to love them. After the decision is made, you act on your love by *demonstrating* it through various acts of kindness. These steps directly contradict how God says you are to love. This is why worldly love is conditional and temporary. Worldly love says, "If you disappoint me, hurt me, or don't meet my expectations, I will withdraw the desire, decision, and demonstration of my love."

GOD'S WAY OF LOVING

As Christians, we know what God's Word says about love. We know it is a must, but we continue to struggle with it. Why? Because we are still operating according to what the world says about love. But if we are truly going to love and forgive as God loves and forgives, we must make some changes and do it God's way. This involves **a decision**, **demonstration**, **desire**, and **determination**. God's way of loving begins with a *decision*. This decision is made out of obedience to God's Word (Matthew 5:44; John 14:15, 23; 15:12, 17; 1 Peter 1:22; 1 John 3:11; 4:7, 21). It is a choice to do what God says. This means despite how you may feel, you will make the choice to love, not necessarily because you desire to, but because you desire to do what pleases God. After the decision to love has been made, it is then *demonstrated* through deeds (1 John 3:18). True love is demonstrated just as God demonstrated His love for us by sacrificing His son. Your love may be demonstrated by any number of ways. However, you can start by praying for the individual. Yes, this may be difficult at first because you will be putting to death your selfish interests and desires. But remember, it is all about obedience to God, and as a Christian you must die daily (Galatians 2:20; 5:24; Romans 6:2, 6, 11). Once you have made the decision to love and have demonstrated it, you may or may not experience a *desire*, or the "warm fuzzy" feelings often associated with love. Keep in mind that godly love has nothing to do with feelings, but everything to do with obedience. I'm sure Jesus didn't "feel" like dying on the cross for us, but He did it out of obedience (Luke 22:42; John 5:30; Hebrews 10:9). However, your greatest desire should be to please God as you allow the Holy Spirit to operate within you (1 John 3:24; 4:13). As a result of your obedience, God will begin to work on your heart. It will amaze you how over time, you can come to love someone that perhaps you thought you couldn't.

Don't be alarmed if it takes time to get to step three (desire). That's why I must add step four. You must be *determined.* Keep trying and don't give up. God may be using this experience to accomplish great things in your life. Be mindful that your greatest blessings from God are not material things (house, car, job, etc.) which will pass away, but rather the blessings that come as a result of the work that God does on the inside of you. This work is eternal and is the only thing that will matter in the end. Pray for God's will to be done. Pray and ask God to reveal what He is trying to teach you. Continue to seek Him and you will feel His grace rest upon you. When you are tempted to judge, be reminded of how God continues to love you in spite of you. **So what's love got to do with your walk with the Lord? EVERYTHING!**

Text

Romans 5:8 says "But God demonstrates his own love for us in this: While we were still sinners, Christ died for us." This short verse gives the steps to love: demonstration, transformation, and substitution.

Demonstration

God demonstrates his own love toward us . . .

God demonstrated His love toward us. He put His love into action. Love must be extended before it can be received. It is one thing to say you love someone, but when you really mean it, your actions will show it. This is easy when you feel love toward an individual, but remember, love God's way has nothing to do with feelings. Love is a choice. You can choose to love someone even when you don't feel like it. You must do away with all the excuses for why you can't love. You know what they are: "She doesn't love me." "He betrayed me." "She didn't apologize." "I didn't do anything wrong." "They need to come to me." We can come up with as many excuses as there are different circumstances surrounding the estranged relationship.

The inability to love is rooted in self-centeredness. The individual will not move past thinking about self. They are stuck in their own feelings of being wronged, hurt, disappointed, let down, or disrespected. God desires you to let these things go and extend love anyway. "Ouch!" Can you imagine how God must have felt when man fell in the Garden of Eden? Do you think He was hurt, disappointed, rejected, and let down? Yes, He probably felt all of these, but He loved us anyway. "Well, He's God," you might say. Yes, He is, but He has put His Spirit in each one of His children, which gives you the grace and the ability through the Holy Spirit to love just as He does. I heard Cheryl Wesley speak on love. She made four excellent points I would like to share:

1) **You can't love until you really understand who love is.**

   Notice she didn't say *what* love is, but rather *who* love is. You will never know love until you come to understand that God Himself is love. Love is not a part of His personality. Personalities change. A person can be one way one day and another way the next day. Love is God's character. Character is the way a person is at the core, when no one is looking. It is real, genuine, constant, and consistent. God *is* love. It is not a part of Him, it is Him.

2) **You can't love until you have accepted the love of Christ.**

   You will never be able to love God's way until you have accepted the love of Christ in your heart. Although God extends His love toward you, it is up to you to accept it. Revelation 3:20 says, "Here I am! I stand at the door and knock. If anyone hears my voice and opens the door, I will come in and eat with him . . ." God is standing at the door knocking. He desires to come into your heart, but you must open the door. It is your choice to accept the love gift God has for you.

3) **You can't love until you have seen yourself as God sees you.**

   It is important that we look at ourselves as God sees us. Why? Because God sees all the things that no one else can see. He sees our shortcomings, downfalls, frailties, and imperfections. There are times we may have a tendency to overlook our faults, which can cause us to put ourselves on a pedestal. When we put ourselves on a pedestal, we can become judgmental of others. We tend to see everyone else's faults, but never our own. Looking at yourself as God sees you is a humbling experience. Isaiah said, "Woe to me! I am ruined! For I am a man of unclean lips, and I live among a people of unclean lips . . ." (Isaiah 6:5). As Isaiah looked at himself through the eyes of God; he humbled himself and saw some things he did not like and it changed his perspective.

4) **You can't love others until you first love yourself.**

   Matthew 19:19 says to "love your neighbor as yourself." Perhaps God said this because He knew many of us would not have a problem loving ourselves. However, you must keep all things in right perspective. The Word of God also says that you should not think more highly of yourself than you ought to think (Romans 12:3). I believe God is saying, just as you would take care of yourself and not hurt yourself, you should do the same for one another. You should provide for others, take care of others, be kind to others, and love others, just as you would yourself.

God is calling for you to demonstrate your love for others just as He demonstrated His love toward you.

DISCUSSION QUESTIONS

1) Explain your biblical understanding of love.

_____

_____

_____

_____

_____

2) Do you demonstrate love the way God desires?

_____

_____

_____

_____

_____

3) What can you do to allow God's love to shine through you?

_____

_____

_____

_____

_____

TRANSFORMATION

. . . while we were yet sinners . . .

Not only did God demonstrate His love toward us, but He did so when we were in our worst state. Man sinned and separated himself from God. We were in bad condition. You might say we were lower than low and we needed to be reconciled to God. Although man was in an ugly state, God saw us in our transformed state. He saw us for what we could become. He didn't focus on where we were, but recognized where we could be through His grace.

As you seek to love others, you must view them in their transformed state. Yes, they may be mean and unloving, but you must look at them through the eyes of the Father and see them for what they can become. It is easier to love when you look through the eyes of God and see how He loves you, even in your worst state. His love is a transforming love, a love that changes you into what He desires you to be.

DISCUSSION QUESTIONS

1) Is it sometimes difficult for you to love? Why? Why not?

_____

_____

_____

_____

_____

_____

_____

_____

_____

2) How might seeing people as God sees them help you to love them?

_____

_____

_____

_____

_____

_____

_____

_____

_____

SUBSTITUTION

. . . Christ died for us.

Christ died for our sins. Although He knew no sin, He willingly paid the price for ours. It should have been you and I on the cross, but Jesus humbly and obediently sacrificed His life and received our death penalty. Generally, you and I are not asked to die for one another, but the question is, what are you willing to sacrifice for others? What are you willing to do for others? Love is not selfish, it gives. Love requires you to sacrifice yourself. It means many times, putting others before yourself. Real love moves from selfishness to selflessness. When you experience relationship problems, whether in marriage or friendship, it is usually the result of selfishness. Each individual is consumed with themselves, their feelings, their desires, their disappointments, and their personal agenda. God's love calls for you to move from self and see the needs of others. As you see the needs of others, you must trust God to meet your needs.

DISCUSSION QUESTIONS

1) How does God's sacrifice of His only son apply to your love for others?

_____

_____

_____

_____

_____

_____

_____

_____

2) What are you willing to sacrifice for others?

_____

_____

_____

_____

_____

_____

_____

_____

WHAT ABOUT FORGIVENESS?

We cannot talk about love without talking about forgiveness. In my view, they go hand in hand. As you engage in relationships, it is inevitable that disappointments will surface. As difficult as this may be, you will find yourself in a situation where you need to forgive. For some, this may be very difficult. The level of difficulty may depend on the level of hurt or offense. I cannot stress enough that in order to live a victorious life, forgiveness is a must. There are two reasons why I say this. First, you should forgive because Christ has forgiven you. Ephesians 4:32 says, ". . . be kind and compassionate to one another, forgiving each other, just as in Christ God forgave you." You forgive because God forgives. As discussed earlier, you forgive, not necessarily because you want to, like to, or feel like it, but you forgive out of obedience to God. Second, you should forgive because unforgiveness gives Satan a stronghold in your life. In 2 Corinthians 2:10–11, Paul tells us, "If you forgive anyone, I also forgive him. And what I have forgiven—if there was anything to forgive—I have forgiven in the sight of Christ for your sake, in order that Satan might not outwit us. For we are not unaware of his schemes." Yes, the unwillingness to forgive is a device Satan uses to keep you locked up in bitterness and hatred. It prevents you from growing in Christ: it stifles your walk with the Lord. Yes, you are still saved, but it takes away your joy and peace. It steals your victory. Forgiveness may be easier said than done, but it can be done!

HOW DO I FORGIVE?

I would like to share the steps to forgiveness from Neil T. Anderson's book, *The Steps to Freedom in Christ*. I have found them to be most helpful, liberating, and practical.

STEP 1) Forgiveness does not mean you forget

Forgiveness does not mean that you acquire amnesia and forget the hurt that someone has caused you. It does not mean you will have no recollection and will be unable to recall how you were offended. What it does mean is that you will choose to not hold the offense against the person who offended you. How do you do that? By not bringing the issue up every time you see the individual, or better yet, even allowing it to come to mind. You see this often in a marital relationship. A couple has an argument and one or both parties bring up past wrongs of the other individual. True forgiveness does what God does. He casts your sins into the sea of forgetfulness (Micah 7:19). He forgives and cleanses you (1 John 1:9). He washes the slate clean as if you had never sinned. You too must wipe the slate clean and cast the offenses of others into the sea of forgetfulness. You must not hold unforgiveness in your heart, but release the individual from their offense; thus, releasing yourself from bondage.

STEP 2) Forgiveness involves making a choice

Just as love is a choice, forgiveness is also a choice. Like love, it is a choice that is made out of obedience to God. There are many reasons we give for not forgiving and many of them may seem valid. But you have to push aside what you want, what you feel, how wrong the other person is, and decide to forgive no matter what. Please hear me out. I am not saying forgiveness is easy. In fact it can be very difficult, but keep in mind that God would never ask you to do something that He would not give you the ability to do.

STEP 3) Forgiveness is between you and God, not you and the other person

When you recognize that forgiveness has nothing to do with the person you are forgiving, and realize that it is between you and God, it is easier to forgive. Allow your desire to be in the will of God and to be obedient to Him, to supersede your hurt, anger and bitterness. More than anything, you must remain focused on the eternal reality, which is not always apparent in the physical realm. As Christians, our goal is one day to see Jesus face to face. Yes, heaven is our goal and Satan will use broken relationships to get our focus off our goal. The Christian's life is guided by the desire to live a life that is pleasing to God, with the hope of our eternal destination—heaven. You forgive with this in mind.

STEP 4) Forgiveness is agreeing to live with the consequences of the other person's sin

Quite frankly, we have no choice but to live with the consequences of another person's sin. Most times, we cannot change the situation when someone has hurt us. If that were possible then we would never be hurt. We can however, choose how we will live with the consequences of another's sin. We can choose to live in bitterness and unforgiveness, or we can choose to live in peace and forgiveness. I don't know about you, but I would much rather live in peace and forgiveness. Forgiveness will cost us something. Once again, just as love is sacrificial, so is forgiveness. Remember, Jesus set the example. He died on the cross so that we could freely receive the forgiveness of our sins.

STEP 5) Acknowledge the hurt

Please understand, I am not advocating that you should not hurt or that you should be in denial about the pain you feel. Being hurt is inevitable and it is real. You cannot hide your feelings under a rug and keep going as if nothing ever happened. The healing process can only begin when you acknowledge your hurt and hate. Does this mean you acknowledge it to the individual who has wronged you? Maybe, maybe not. This is not always possible. The individual may be deceased or perhaps you have lost contact. When the person is accessible, it may not always be wise. The individual may not respond responsibly and confrontation could make matters worse. You must pray and determine if facing the individual is the best thing to do. What matters most is that you first acknowledge the hurt and hate to yourself and then take it to God. It is okay to cry out to the Lord and tell Him how you feel. First Peter 5:7 says you can cast your cares upon Him for He cares for you. You serve a loving God who comforts in times of distress.

STEP 6) Don't wait until you feel like forgiving

Once again, I must compare forgiveness with love. Like love, forgiveness is not based upon feelings. As we shared earlier, it is a choice you make out of obedience to God. You may never feel like forgiving. To be honest, you may have all kinds of excuses for not forgiving, and many of them will be justifiable. Start by making the decision to forgive. It is a conscious choice. Once you take that step, God will work on your heart and the feelings of hurt and hate will gently fade; and love and forgiveness will abide.

I would like to add another step, which I have found to be very important.

STEP 7) Continue to pray and don't allow Satan to creep back in

This step is critical because if you are not careful, Satan will creep right back into your heart and you will find yourself walking in bitterness all over again. You must guard your heart. Galatians 5:1 says to "Stand firm, then, and do not let yourselves be burdened again by a yoke of slavery." Although Paul was dealing with freedom from the bondage of the law, he lets you know that you can, if you are not careful, find yourself back in bondage after you have been set free. You must stand fast, stay in the Word, and continue in prayer. Your enemy, the devil, prowls around like a roaring lion looking for someone to devour (1 Peter 5:8). Satan will use any open wound to take you back where you started.

DISCUSSION QUESTIONS

1) Have you been holding unforgiveness in your heart?

_____

_____

_____

_____

_____

2) If yes, how has it affected your life?

_____

_____

_____

_____

_____

3) You can be set free today. Are you willing to take Anderson's steps to freedom?

_____

_____

_____

_____

_____

Perhaps you have read this lesson and thought to yourself, "I can't do this." I want to assure you, you can. Loving difficult individuals and forgiving those who have hurt you is not easy, but when your heart is sincere and you desire to do it, God will enable you to do what you thought you could never do. Ask Him to help you. He said if you ask anything according to His will, He hears you (1 John 5:14). Love and forgiveness are His will and because of that He will give you the desires of your heart (Psalm 37:4). Be determined to love and forgive. Don't give up until you get there.

Anderson recommends that after you have completed all the steps that you pray and list each individual you desire to forgive. He encourages you to say, "Lord, I forgive (name) for (offense)." You may only have one individual or you may have a list of 10. However many there may be, give each one to God. Make your statement an affirmative, "I forgive" rather than "I'm going to forgive" or "I want to forgive." Be determined to be set free and walk in victory. You can do it!

As I close out this lesson on love and forgiveness, I am reminded of Galatians 6:10, that says, "Therefore, as we have opportunity, let us do good to all people, especially to those who belong to the family of believers." Paul is reminding us that as Christians, we have the responsibility to do good unto everyone, not just those we like, those who are good to us, those we know, or those of our race, but we are challenged to love everyone. He says, "As we have opportunity . . ." In other words, every time you get a chance you should show love. Why? Because this is how you reflect Christ. Others are drawn to the Lord when they see the love of Christ in you (Matthew 5:16). In addition, you may not have the chance tomorrow. So many people live with regrets because they did not choose to forgive someone, show love toward someone or lend a helping hand when they had the opportunity, and now it is too late. I urge you to give love while you can, extend an act of kindness, or make the choice to forgive. When you do, you will live in peace, knowing you have been obedient to the Father.

God has blessed my husband and I with three beautiful children. They are all different. Not only are they different ages, but they also have different personalities. They have various likes and dislikes. One is very affectionate and loves hugs and kisses. Another likes personal space and doesn't like to be close. One loves to talk and will tell everything, while another is quiet and reserved. They have different friends and interests. Although they are all very different, they all have one thing in common—they all have the same father. Nothing can change the fact that they are sisters and brother. This is what we must remember as we are working to love and forgive. As children of God, we are all different. We have different strengths and weaknesses. We vary in personalities. Some are pleasant and some are not so pleasant. But one thing we must remember—we all have the same Father. God loves us all and as His children, He desires us to love one another. I challenge you to make the choice to love and forgive, because God loves and forgives you.

LESSON 6 – LOVE THAT FORGIVES

Goal: To find liberty and peace through loving and forgiving an individual who has offended you

Homework Assignment:

- Spend some time in prayer and repentance. Ask God to search your heart as it relates to love and forgiveness. Be transparent with God and yourself. If there is a person or persons you need to forgive, take the steps to freedom (Neil T. Anderson). Do not be discouraged if you need to do this more than once. Do it as many times as you need to prevent the enemy from stepping in.

- Remember, sometimes love and forgiveness can be a process.

- Journal what God does in your heart. Share with the group next time.

_____

_____

_____

_____

_____

_____

_____

_____

_____

_____

_____

_____

Fasting for a Breakthrough

Then Jesus was led by the Spirit into the desert to be tempted by the devil. After fasting forty days and forty nights, he was hungry (Matthew 4:1–2).

We live in a society that thrives on the thought, "If it feels good, do it." A popular recording artist once sang, "It's yo' thang, do whatcha wanna do." Many live life from day to day motivated by instant gratification. With no regard for the Word of God, they make decisions based on what feels right at the moment. They walk according to the flesh and not the Spirit (Galatians 5:1). However, it is important to know when you fast, you bring flesh into subjection, causing it to fall in line with God. It sets your attention on the things of God and enables you to place things in proper perspective—a spiritual perspective. Often fasting is related to going without food for a specified period of time. The Bible speaks frequently of this type of fast. However, fasting can involve the sacrifice of anything in your life that is significant to you. God is concerned with you bringing into subjection those areas in your life that are controlling you, as well as areas you have not yielded to Him.

WHAT IS FASTING?

Let us examine what fasting is not, before we state what fasting is. Fasting is not abstaining from food in order to lose weight, to cleanse the body's system, or to gain attention from others. Fasting is going without a physical desire or need, for a spiritual purpose. Food happens to be essential to life. Not only do you need it, but I'm willing to say most of us love it. At times we crave it, not to mention over indulge in it. It is something you need, and desire. Because of this, it brings God glory to see you sacrifice food (an essential need and deep desire), for something spiritual (a greater need and greater desire). The Bible says, ". . . man does not live on bread alone but on every word that comes from the mouth of the Lord" (Deuteronomy 8:3; Matthew 4:4; Luke 4:4). In other words, your survival is not solely dependent upon food, but there is something greater and deeper that sustains you—the Word of God. Fasting is a spiritual discipline that moves the hand of God. It is a great exchange that involves giving God what means most to you and receiving something greater in the spirit. When you do this, God has to respond.

FASTING FOR A BREAKTHROUGH

Now that we have discussed what fasting is, we must answer the question, "What is a breakthrough?" As I stated previously, God responds to fasting. He is moved to act when you fast. It has been said that fasting is a 911 call to God and gets His attention, but Dr. W. Hulitt Gloer, of Truett Theological Seminary shares that it might be more accurate to say that "Fasting gets our attention. We have God's attention, but He may not have ours." For those who are parents, you understand that your child has different cries. Because you know your child, you can instinctively identify your child's cries. You can immediately distinguish whether it is a wet cry, a hungry cry, a tired and sleepy cry, or a cry of intense pain. As a loving parent, you respond differently to each cry. In addition to responding differently to various cries, your response time is different, according to which cry it may be. You may prolong your response time if they are crying because they are irritable. However, if it is a cry of intense pain, you respond immediately. That's what I believe fasting is and does. It is your cry of intense pain and need for God, which triggers an immediate response from Him.

Does this mean that every time I fast, God is going to change my situation? Is He going to move in the way I need Him to? Is my breakthrough going to be what I am praying and asking Him for? Maybe, maybe not. Breakthrough is not defined as getting what you think you need or want from God through fasting. Your breakthrough comes when God ministers to you as a result of your fast. The Bible says in Matthew 4, that after Jesus had fasted for forty days and forty nights, and was tempted of the devil, the devil left Him and angels came and ministered to Him (Matthew 4:11). God ministers to you through your fasting. He may or may not change your situation, but in fasting you gain peace in the midst of the storm.

The exchange that occurs in fasting is not flesh for flesh; but rather, flesh for Spirit. What you receive through fasting is strictly spiritual. You must understand that fasting takes you out of the physical realm and places you in the spiritual realm where you make God and your relationship with Him your only priority.

ARE WE COMMANDED TO FAST?

Fasting is not given as a commandment. However, it is a spiritual discipline that is acknowledged throughout the Bible. Esther (Esther 4:16), Daniel (Daniel 10:3), Paul (Acts 9:9), Anna (Luke 2:37), Cornelius (Acts 10:30), Samuel (1 Samuel 7:1–8), Elijah (1 Kings 19: 2–18), John the Baptist (Matthew 3:4; Luke 1:15) and Jesus Himself (Matthew 4; Luke 4:2) fasted. Not only does the Bible speak of personal, individual fasts, but it also speaks of public fasts, when groups of people would fast together (Leviticus 23:27; Joel 2:15; 2 Chronicles 20:1–4, Ezra 8:21–23).

Jesus gave instructions concerning fasting in Matthew 6. Fasting should be a private matter between you and God. You should not walk around looking as though you are about to faint, bringing attention upon yourself, but "put oil on your head and wash your face" (Matthew 6:17). In other words, give God glory in your very appearance.

WHAT DOES FASTING INVOLVE?

As we discussed earlier, fasting can involve any number of things. It is giving up something in the flesh for something greater in the spirit. The something in the flesh can be anything you deeply need or desire. It could be the television, a particular food (meat, sweets, etc.), certain people, sexual intimacy in marriage (will be discussed next) and so on. I believe God desires you to sacrifice, and even crucify, those areas in your life that are getting in the way of your relationship with Him. Although food is generally thought of when discussing fasting, it can include so many other areas in your life.

FASTING FROM SEXUAL INTIMACY

First Corinthians 7:1–5 addresses fasting within the marital context. Of course, if you are single, you are to abstain from sexual intimacy at all times (1 Corinthians 6:18; 1 Thessalonians 4:3–4). However, it is permissible, within the marital relationship to fast from sexual intimacy, with the condition that both the husband and the wife are in agreement and it is for the purpose of spiritual communion with God through a temporary period of fasting and prayer.

WHAT DO I DO WHEN I GET HUNGRY?

Fasting is not easy. It's not supposed to be easy. If it were, it wouldn't be a sacrifice. You must understand, just as Jesus was tempted during His fast, you too will be tempted. The hunger pangs will come. The thought of food will exist. Cookies and cakes will appear from nowhere. You will get to work and find your co-workers decided to have a potluck lunch. The enemy has his way of trying to prevent you from fasting because he knows the power you will gain as a result. But understand that your breakthrough comes when you don't yield. When you find yourself getting weak, pray and ask God for strength. Quote Scriptures or read the Word. This is what makes fasting so powerful. Every hunger pang is a reminder to pray (commune with God), acknowledge your need for Him (humble yourself), view your situation through spiritual lens (focus on God), and defeat the enemy. I promise you, when you do these things, just like in Matthew 4:11, when Satan left Jesus, he will also leave you. You will win through fasting.

CAN I DRINK LIQUIDS?

There are many different opinions about whether liquids are permitted during a fast. Some say yes, some say no; many say only water is permissible. Richard Foster (1998) states in *Celebration of Discipline* that because Matthew 4:2 says after Jesus had fasted forty days and forty nights He was hungry, meant He drank water, because the Scriptures do not mention Him being thirsty. I would like to submit that more than anything, fasting is personal and the Holy Spirit will guide you in what sacrifice He wants you to make.

HOW LONG SHOULD I FAST?

This is a personal and individual question. The Bible does not give a specific amount of time that you should fast. My answer is that your fast should be for whatever length of time is a sacrifice for you. God is not as concerned about the length of time you fast, as He is about it being a genuine, authentic sacrifice. God was not pleased with Cain's offering because it was not a sacrifice for him (Genesis 4:1–7). The length of your fast should be determined by what is actually a real sacrifice for you. For some that may be a half-day, for another it may be three days. For someone else it may be one meal. You must determine the length of the fast for yourself and allow that to be between you and God. Only you know whether God is pleased with your sacrifice. A person that is new to fasting may first fast for shorter periods of time and increase as they grow in this spiritual discipline. Those who have illnesses or may be on medication that requires food should use discretion.

THE RESULTS OF FASTING

Communion with God

Fasting and prayer draws you closer to God and when you draw closer to Him, He draws closer to you (James 4:8). Why? Because prayer is communication with God and as you speak to Him, He speaks to you. He will speak to you about you and your situation. He will bring His Word to your remembrance. His voice becomes clearer to you as you remove the "smog" of flesh and set your attention on Him.

Humility

Fasting humbles you. With your physical need for food being unmet, you come to realize your dependence on God for everything. You acknowledge that you need God, even to get through the time of fasting. Jesus taught the disciples to pray, "Give us each day our daily bread" (Luke 11:3). Jesus was not only speaking of physical food, but He was also speaking of spiritual food. He was talking about divine supplies. Through fasting, you acknowledge that without God you are nothing, can do nothing and can be nothing. You need Him as provider and sustainer.

Keeps Your Focus on God

Fasting changes your perspective on things. It becomes your spiritual lens through which you view everything. It keeps God and spiritual matters at the forefront of your mind. As you go through your daily activities, it helps you to see your problems, challenges, and situations as God sees them. Because fasting takes you to a higher level spiritually, your view of your problems change. They seem smaller. They don't appear insurmountable. They don't weigh you down. Fasting reminds you to focus on God and to set your affections on things above and not on things of this earth (Colossians 3:2).

Gives You Victory over the Enemy

Fasting gives you power over the enemy. "How can I be victorious over Satan when I am fatigued from fasting?" you might ask. When you are fasting, you do not operate according to your own strength. First Corinthians 4:10 tells us we are weak, but God is strong. You become strong through Him. Jesus was victorious over Satan after fasting in Matthew 4. God gave Him strength through His Word. Fasting reminds you to use the Word of God as your weapon and not attempt to fight the battle yourself. "For our struggle is not against flesh and blood, but against the rulers, against the authorities, against the powers of this dark world and against the spiritual forces of evil in the heavenly realms" (Ephesians 6:12).

Brings You to a Place of Submission and Obedience

Fasting is an act of self-denial and mortification of the flesh. It is saying to God, "Lord, I want You more than this." When you are able to bring the flesh under subjection through fasting, it becomes easier to bring other areas of your life under subjection, whether it is lying, drinking, jealousy, unforgiveness, adultery, or any other sin. When you learn to rely on God for strength in the area of the physical need for food, you can learn to rely on Him for strength in areas of sin in your life.

THE HEART OF THE MATTER

More than anything during your fast, God is concerned with the condition of the heart. He wants a heart that is yielded to Him. He wants your worship to be true and pure. Fasting should not become a ritual that you perform to obtain favor from God, to get the attention of man or to make yourself feel holy. The decision to fast should be internally motivated and should yield external results. Isaiah 58 gives an excellent picture of what God desires in your fast. Take a few moments to read it.

DISCUSSION QUESTIONS

1) Read Isaiah 58 and make a list of what God wants and does not want in your fast.

_____

_____

_____

_____

_____

_____

_____

_____

2) Make a list of what God promises to do when you fast with a pure heart.

_____

_____

_____

_____

_____

_____

_____

_____

God explicitly lets you know in Isaiah 58 what He does and does not desire in your fast. During Isaiah's day, God's people were coming to the temple for worship. They were fasting, and worshipping, but yet they continued to oppress their workers. They continued to spread vicious rumors and fight among themselves. In other words, their worship was not true. Although they did all the right things outwardly, inwardly there had been no change. When you fast, God is most concerned with what is going on inside you. He wants to see a change of heart. This inward change will manifest itself outwardly. Verse 6 of Isaiah 58 says that the kind of fast that is pleasing to God is a fast that calls you "to loose the chains of injustice and untie the cords of the yoke, to set the oppressed free and break every yoke." It goes on in verse 7 saying, shouldn't you feed the hungry and care for the poor? Clothe the naked? When fasting comes from a genuine heart, it produces fruit.

What a blessing you receive when you fast with the right motivations and the right heart. Isaiah 58:8 says when you do these things, your salvation will come. Your healing will come. The glory of the Lord will protect you and the Lord will answer you. Your light will shine out from the darkness. The Lord will guide you and satisfy you in drought. He will make you as a watered garden that never gets dry. Yes, fasting benefits your personal walk with the Lord, but God desires a fast that goes beyond yourself. He wants a fast that produces fruit and makes a difference in the lives of others.

In a world that bombards you with thoughts to have your own way and to do your own thing, God is calling for His children to live a life of sacrifice and obedience. Fasting tells God He is the priority in your life. Mature Christians recognize that there is more to life than what the eye can see and that there is a spiritual realm you must hunger to experience. The temptation to walk by sight is resisted. As a result, a higher level of living is experienced. God wants you to genuinely offer Him the sacrifice of your very being—to lay your all on the altar. However, it doesn't stop there. God is truly glorified when your sacrifice, which begins inwardly, spills over to those around you. It is then and only then that you receive your breakthrough.

DISCUSSION QUESTIONS

1) What is in your life that may be getting in the way of your relationship with God that you may need to sacrifice?

_____

_____

_____

_____

2) Review the list of results from fasting. What other results might you experience in your life as a result of fasting?

_____

_____

_____

_____

3) What can you do during your fast to help you be victorious and to prevent yielding to the temptations Satan puts before you?

_____

_____

_____

_____

4) What can you do to produce more fruit as a result of your fast?

_____

_____

_____

_____

LESSON 7 – FASTING FOR A BREAKTHROUGH

Goal: To establish the spiritual discipline of fasting for the purpose of spiritual growth and communion with God

Homework Assignment:

- Designate a specific day and time of fasting as a group with your Victorious Disciples sisters.

- Designate a specific day and time for a personal fast.

- Commit this time to communion with God through reading the Word, prayer and listening to His voice.

- Journal your experience and record what God speaks to you. Share with the group next time.

_____

_____

_____

_____

_____

_____

_____

_____

_____

_____

_____

_____

Created for Worship

But only one thing is needed. Mary has chosen what is better, and it will not be taken away from her (Luke 10:42).

God created humankind for the purpose of having a relationship and communion with Him. Everything about God is centered around relationship. God the Father, Son, and Holy Ghost have a Trinitarian relationship, being one God in three persons. He created us with a longing for a loving relationship with Him and with others. When our fellowship with Him was broken by the fall, He sent Jesus to die for our sins, for the purpose of restoring our broken relationship and fellowship with Him. God says in His Word that He is a jealous God (Exodus 20:5; 34:14) and that we should have no other gods before Him (Exodus 20:3). He lets us know that He desires to have a one-on-one, personal relationship with us. What am I trying to say? I'm saying God wants us to worship Him. When we worship God, we open the door to an intimate fellowship with Him that takes our relationship to another level.

There was a time when I thought worshipping God was merely going to church every Sunday. If someone were to ask me how do you worship God? My answer would have been, "By going to church." While going to church is a part of worship, it is a small part of what worship really is. Worship begins in the heart and flows outward. For the Christian, worship should be a lifestyle. Your private, daily worship should pour out into your public worship and church attendance. But before we begin to talk about how we worship God, let's first define what worship is.

Worship is a conversation between God and humankind. We communicate with God and He communicates with us. Worship involves giving God our all. It is the purpose of our eternal calling. Worship is an expression of our love and adoration toward God. Worship involves magnifying God with everything within us—body, soul and spirit. In worship, we pour out our hearts to our Lord, Jesus Christ. Worship involves love, obedience, and sacrifice. I must say, as I attempt to define worship, I find it difficult to find words that provide an adequate description. Morris Smith shared, "Real worship defies definition; it can only be experienced." God never intended for His children to come to know worship by reading about it or talking about it, but God desires for us to *experience* worship and communion with Him. Jesus told the Samaritan woman at the well that "a time is coming and has now come when the true worshippers will worship the Father in spirit and truth, for they are the kind of worshippers the Father seeks. God is spirit, and his worshippers must worship in spirit and in truth" (John 4:23–24).

In Luke 10 we find the story of two sisters, Mary and Martha, who teach us five valuable lessons about worship: Worship involves getting personal with God, worship involves getting into the presence of God, worship involves making God the first priority, worship is permanent, and worship might cause you problems.

Worship Involves Getting Personal With God

Mary and Martha had a personal relationship with Jesus. It was Jesus they called when their brother Lazarus was sick unto death. John 11:5 reports that Jesus loved Martha, Mary, and Lazarus. Now, in Luke 10, Jesus is at Martha's house. Therefore, I believe it is safe to say they knew Jesus and Jesus knew them. As a result, Mary was able to sit at His feet and pour out her heart to Him because she had a close relationship with Him. You cannot worship a God you do not know and you cannot worship a God you only know about. You must have a personal relationship with God to worship Him. It is not enough that your parents and grandparents worshipped Him. You must establish an intimate relationship with Him for yourself.

While anyone and anything can praise God, only those who know Him as personal Savior can worship Him. The Bible says nature praises God. The mountains, hills, trees, valleys, and seas (Isaiah 44:23; Isaiah 55:12; Psalm 65:13; Psalm 69:34) all praise God. Jesus told the Pharisees even the rocks will cry out if the disciples should hold their peace (Luke 19:40). While anyone and anything can praise God, worship involves communion, fellowship, and relationship. This comes about by knowing God, and you come to know Him through His Word. It is through His Word that God reveals Himself to you. In the Old Testament, God revealed Himself through experiences. As individuals experienced God in various ways, they would ascribe a name to Him, which characterized the experience.

When God told Abraham to offer Isaac as a sacrifice, Abraham was obedient (Genesis 22). He took his only son Isaac, and prepared to kill him. Just as he stretched forth his hand to slay his son, an angel of the Lord spoke and told him not to harm him. Abraham looked up and seeing a ram in the bush, he responded, "Jehovah Jireh" (the Lord will provide). When God delivered the children of Israel from the hands of Amalek in Exodus 17, Moses built an altar and said, "Jehovah Nissi" (the Lord is my banner). In Judges 6, when Gideon feared the attack of the Midianites, he made a sacrifice unto God. An angel appeared to Gideon and told him he did not have to fear, "I am with you," the angel said. Gideon responded with, "Jehovah Shalom" (You are my peace). As the people of God worshipped Him, God revealed Himself to them in a greater way. Their experiences brought them to a deeper level in their walk with the Lord.

I am reminded of Exodus 3:14, when God told Moses to bring the children of Israel out of Egypt. Moses questioned God and asked what he should tell the children of Israel when they inquired about the name of his God. God said, tell them, "I AM that I AM sent you." In other words, God was saying, "Moses, I am whatever you need." There is a strong message in that word for you today. Whatever you need, God is. Today, I may need Him as Jehovah Rapha, my healer. Tomorrow you may need Him as Jehovah Eli, your guide. The next day we may need Him as Jehovah Tsidkenu, our righteousness. The point is, God is for you, whatever you need and whenever you need it. That's good news!

As you come to know God in a personal, intimate way, you will come to experience God in ways you have never experienced before. As He reveals more and more of Himself to you, you will see that He is whatever you may need Him to be at any given time and in any given situation.

DISCUSSION QUESTIONS

1) Describe your relationship/fellowship with Jesus Christ?

_____

_____

_____

_____

_____

_____

_____

2) Has your relationship with Jesus grown in the past few months/years? Explain.

_____

_____

_____

_____

_____

_____

_____

WORSHIP INVOLVES GETTING INTO THE PRESENCE OF GOD

We Want His Presents but Not His Presence

While Martha was busy taking care of other things, Mary got into the presence of God. She sat at Jesus' feet and focused solely on Him. This is what God desires from us. He wants us to spend time in His presence, not necessarily because we want anything from Him, but because we want more of Him. A few years ago my family and I went to the state fair, which is held in our city each year. We left the house as a family, drove to the park as a family, parked the car and walked into the park as a family. Once we entered the park, our oldest daughter, who was about 14 at the time, asked her dad for some money (she knew she would get more by asking him instead of me). Just as she knew he would, he reached into his pocket and generously gave her money. She then pointed across the walkway where her friends were standing and asked if she could go with them. Her dad and I looked at each other. How naive of us to think our teenage daughter would desire to attend the state fair with her parents and younger siblings. My husband said, "Our little girl has reached the age where she wants our *presents*, but she doesn't want our *presence*." Many times this is the message we send to God. We want His presents—all the things He can give us: the car, the house, the job, a family, good health, and so on. However, we don't want His presence. We don't want to spend time with Him. We don't want to study His Word or live our lives by His principles. You must remember the Bible tells you to "seek first his kingdom and his righteousness, and all these things will be given to you as well" (Matthew 6:33). When you seek God's *presence* He will then bless you with His *presents*.

Go Where He Is

In the Old Testament, worship was centralized. Tabernacles were constructed and taken from place to place for worship. The Holy Spirit, however, abolished the old system of worship. Jesus told the woman at the well in John 4:21, ". . . a time is coming when you will worship the Father neither on this mountain nor in Jerusalem." In other words, Jesus was saying the time will come when you will no longer have to come to Jerusalem to worship the Father. That time came when the Holy Spirit descended on the day of Pentecost. Now, as children of God, we have the Holy Spirit within us, which enables us to worship God wherever we are. Our bodies are the temple of God (1 Corinthians 6:19). God is not locked into any location, but we can praise Him anywhere and at anytime. Sometimes as I'm driving down the street, I worship God in my car. At other times, I am in my home and I stop to worship Him. We can worship God anytime and anywhere. That's good news!

Take Something with You

Worship requires that you take something with you. Once again, during Old Testament times, the people were required to bring animal sacrifices. A blood sacrifice was necessary for the atonement of sins (Hebrews 9:22). However, when Jesus died for your sins, He became your sacrifice. No longer do you have to gather annually to offer sacrifices for forgiveness of sins. "But when this priest had offered for all time one sacrifice for sins, he sat down at the right hand of God" (Hebrews 10:12). Although God no longer requires a blood sacrifice for the remission of sins, He does desire for you to bring something to Him when you worship. He desires a sacrifice of a different kind. What does God want you to sacrifice? God desires for you to sacrifice that which is most important to you. It might be your spouse, your children, your job, your pride, unforgiveness, selfishness, or anything that is interfering with your walk with the Lord. God wants you to give it to Him. Worship always involves sacrifice and obedience. That's why Hebrews 13:15–16 says, ". . . let us continually offer to God a sacrifice of praise—the fruit of lips that confess his name. And do not forget to do good and to share with others, for with such sacrifices God is pleased." Romans 12:1 says "Therefore, I urge you, brothers, in view of God's mercy, to offer your bodies as living sacrifices, holy and pleasing to God—this is your spiritual act of worship." God desires for you to offer yourself as a sacrifice to Him. He desires a life that is totally yielded to Him for His glory and His purpose.

DISCUSSION QUESTIONS

1) If you were to describe most of your encounters with God, would you say that you seek His *presents* or *presence*? Explain.

_____

_____

_____

2) When you hear the word "worship" what comes to your mind?

_____

_____

_____

3) Has worship become a lifestyle for you or is it something you only do on Sundays?

_____

_____

_____

4) When was the last time you were alone and decided to worship God?

_____

_____

_____

5) What is presently in your life that is blocking your relationship with God? What do you need to offer as a sacrifice to Him?

_____

_____

_____

Worship Involves Making God The First Priority

Martha was taking care of what *appeared* to be urgent, while Mary was taking care of what was necessary. How many times have you found yourself in this same situation? You go through your daily activities, taking care of all the urgent things that surface in a day: the meetings, the phone calls to return, the children to pick up, the errands you must run. At the end of the day, you look at your schedule and realize you have done everything that was "urgent," but you have omitted that which was necessary—time for your soul. Mary teaches us that worship comes before service. Martha was busy serving. One may have thought this was a priority—after all she was serving Jesus. The lesson here is that sometimes you can be so busy with the Lord's work, that you neglect the Lord. You can forget *why* you are doing *what* you are doing.

Busyness is a trick that Satan uses to influence you to exclude the Lord from your daily life. You find yourself running on fumes because you haven't had time to fill up with God's Word. You have been deceived into thinking that activity is productivity. Therefore, frustration, lack of patience, and anxiety sets in, all because in actuality, you have put God on the back burner. He is no longer the center and the priority of your life. In theory, He is, but in practice, He is not. There are times when I must stop and take inventory of my life to evaluate the stewardship of my time and my relationship with the Lord. I remind myself that if God is first and foremost in my life and my family is second, then they should get more of my time than anything else. There have been times when I have had to let go of some things and/or people in my life. Sometimes they were dear to my heart, but got in the way of my relationship with God. It was a major sacrifice for me, but it was ultimately a blessing as I was able to grow spiritually as I made my time with the Lord the first priority.

DISCUSSION QUESTIONS

1) What have you allowed to get in the way of your relationship with God?

_____

_____

_____

_____

_____

_____

_____

_____

2) What can you do differently to make God the priority in your life?

_____

_____

_____

_____

_____

_____

_____

_____

Worship Is Permanent

Perhaps it isn't your favorite subject to discuss, but have you ever thought about what you would like people to say about you when you die? Most of us at some point or another have considered death. Perhaps you have gone as far as to think about your funeral. What would you like people to say about you at your funeral? I have never attended a funeral where the people discussed the material possessions of the deceased. I've never heard anyone say, "She sure lived in a beautiful home. He had a fine car and was always dressed well." People never mention *where* a person lived, but they do mention *how* a person lived. I've heard people talk about how their lives were impacted by the deceased. They talked about the individual's character. Remember, whatever you want to be said, you must be working on it now. You cannot wait until that day. It will be too late.

All of the material things you focus on in life will pass away. I love to hear the testimonies of people when they share how God has blessed them with material things. They tell how God blessed them with a new home, a promotion on their job, a substantial raise, or a new child. I can rejoice with them. However, the real rejoicing comes when they are able to say, "God changed my heart. I now love someone I once hated. I have forgiveness in my heart now. I have let go of pride." This is eternal. Yes, God wants to bless you materially, but He wants to do a greater work on the inside of you. God's greatest blessings begin on the inside. This is His eternal work that will never fade away.

This is what Jesus was saying when He told Martha in Luke 10:42, ". . . but only one thing is needed. Mary has chosen what is better, and it will not be taken away from her." In other words, Jesus was saying Mary's worship is permanent. I will remember her worship. Martha's work will fade away. After Jesus left Martha's house, her work would no longer be relevant, but Mary's worship would never subside. In Matthew 26:13, Jesus shared with the disciples after they were upset about Mary pouring upon Him the ointment from the alabaster box, ". . . wherever this gospel is preached throughout the world, what she has done will also be told, in memory of her." Once again, Jesus was letting them know that worship is permanent. More than 2000 years have passed and this story is still being told. It is just as relevant today as it was then. Jesus remembers your worship. He remembers every sacrifice, every tear shed, and every act of obedience.

DISCUSSION QUESTIONS

1) What would you like said about you when you die? What are you doing today to impact what will be said about you when you're gone?

———————————————————————————————

———————————————————————————————

———————————————————————————————

———————————————————————————————

———————————————————————————————

2) Does your life reflect a life of material things or a life of worship?

———————————————————————————————

———————————————————————————————

———————————————————————————————

———————————————————————————————

———————————————————————————————

Worship Might Cause You Problems

Martha went to Jesus and complained about being left to serve alone. This is what happens when you are focusing on work rather than worship. You become short tempered and impatient. You begin to focus on self and what is fair and what isn't. Pride begins to take over and you start to operate in the flesh and not the Spirit. How many times have you found yourself in this same predicament? Work without God as the first priority will cause you pain. You will begin to focus on *doing* rather than *being*. Martha went to Jesus because she was upset that Mary was worshipping instead of working. If you are not careful, you will find yourself in this same situation. You will get so caught up with *doing* for God that you forget He is more concerned about you *being* all that you can be for Him.

There will be times when others will not understand your worship. They might talk about you or complain. They may question why you do what you do. But you cannot allow them to discourage you from worshipping the Lord. Luke 6:26 says, "Woe to you when all men speak well of you, for that is how their fathers treated the false prophets." Jesus was letting you know that when you follow the Father, men will speak against you. Every believer in the Bible experienced opposition, including Jesus Himself. Don't be discouraged by this. James said, "Consider it pure joy, my brothers, whenever you face trials of many kinds" (James 1:2). Although your worship may cause you problems at times, you must remember that suffering, criticism, and opposition are all a part of the Christian life. Your goal and priority is to please Christ. Paul said it best in Galatians 1:10, "Am I now trying to win the approval of men, or of God? Or am I trying to please men? If I were still trying to please men, I would not be a servant of Christ."

DISCUSSION QUESTIONS

1) Have you ever found yourself focusing more on work than worship? If so, what was the result?

_____

_____

_____

_____

_____

2) Have you ever been criticized by others because you found pleasure in worshipping God? If so, how did you handle it?

_____

_____

_____

_____

_____

3) Read the conclusion. Have you made worship a lifestyle or is it something you do only at a designated time and place (Sunday worship service)?

_____

_____

_____

_____

_____

4) What can you do to make worship your *lifestyle* rather than making worship something you *do*?

_____

_____

_____

_____

Continue to make worship a lifestyle. It should be a part of who you are. Worship is not only expressed through traditional methods of prayer, music, singing, playing of instruments, the Scriptures, dancing, clapping, shouting, kneeling, lifting of hands, bowing, lying prostrate, through tears, the Lord's supper, and hearing the Word preached, but worship also involves sharing your testimony, listening to the testimonies of others, being obedient to God's Word, loving others, choosing to do the right thing, walking in the Spirit rather than being overtaken by the flesh, and acknowledging God in your daily decisions. Worship involves your total being; it should be expressed *in* you and *through* you at all times.

LESSON 8 – CREATED FOR WORSHIP

Goal: To establish worship as a lifestyle

Homework Assignment:

- Make consistent time for private worship.

- Make the choice to worship God freely and openly in corporate worship service.

- Make a list of how you can make worship a lifestyle and practice it.

- Journal your experience and share with the group next time.

_____

_____

_____

_____

_____

_____

_____

_____

_____

_____

_____

_____

_____

_____

Empowered by the Holy Spirit

But you will receive power when the Holy Spirit comes on you; and you will be my witnesses in Jerusalem, and in all Judea and Samaria, and to the ends of the earth (Acts 1:8).

As we conclude our *Victorious Disciples* study, we must seal it with a lesson on the Holy Spirit. Everything you have learned in this study, such as knowing who you are in Christ, how to study the Bible, how to have faith, how to grow your prayer life, how to win in spiritual warfare, how to love, forgive, worship and fast, cannot be achieved apart from the Holy Spirit. You cannot be victorious in your walk with the Lord without the Holy Spirit. It is the Holy Spirit who empowers you to do what God has called you to do. Billy Graham states, ". . . if we wish to be men and women who can live victoriously, we need this two-sided gift God has offered us: first, the work of the Son of God *for* us; second, the work of the Spirit of God *in* us" (Graham, 312).

There are many misconceptions about the Holy Spirit. I'd like to dispel three of the major ones. First, many refer to the Holy Spirit as *it*. You must understand the Holy Spirit is not an *it*, but the Holy Spirit is a person. The Bible teaches that the Holy Spirit is a living being. He is the third person in the Godhead—God the Father, God the Son, and God the Holy Spirit. Jesus never referred to the Holy Spirit as *it*. He spoke of the Holy Spirit in John 14, 15 and 16 as "He," signifying the personhood of the Holy Spirit. Second, many believe it is the Holy Spirit who makes a person shout. This form of worship may be accompanied by verbal praises, such as "Hallelujah! Thank You Jesus. Glory!" There might be dancing, clapping, waving of hands, running, jumping, crying, screaming, and other forms of expressions. This is often referred to as shouting. I remember growing up being taught when someone expressed themselves in such a manner during worship that it was because the Holy Spirit "hit" them. As I have matured in the faith and had such experiences myself, I realize it is not because the Holy Spirit "hit" me. It was a conscious choice I made to worship God in an expressive way. The Bible says that

David danced unashamedly as a form of worship to God (2 Samuel 6:16). There are times when an expressive praise to God is appropriate and due to Him.

The third major misconception about the Holy Spirit is that He only dwells within Pentecostal believers. True, the Pentecostal faith, since its conception, has placed a lot of emphasis on the Holy Spirit with the evidence by speaking in tongues. However, every believer is filled with the Holy Spirit the moment they accept Christ as personal Savior. As Jesus was preparing to end His earthly ministry, He told the disciples, "But I tell you the truth: It is for your good that I am going away. Unless I go away, the Counselor will not come to you; but if I go, I will send him to you" (John 16:7). Jesus said it was to their advantage for Him to leave; His departure was necessary for the coming of the Holy Spirit. He did not say that He would send the Comforter for some believers and not others. He simply said, ". . . if I go, I will send him to you." The Holy Spirit is promised to all who believe on Jesus Christ as Lord. This brings us to our first point.

THE FILLING OF THE HOLY SPIRIT

Just before Jesus left His earthly ministry and ascended into heaven, He told the disciples to tarry in Jerusalem and wait for the promise of the Father (Acts 1:4). As they waited, the Bible says they were all in one accord in prayer and supplication. This included the women, Mary, the mother of Jesus, and His brothers (Acts 1:14). On the day of Pentecost they were filled with the Holy Spirit (Acts 2: 1–4). Today this filling of the Holy Spirit is imparted to every one who accepts Jesus Christ as their personal Savior.

The Holy Spirit Is Your Comforter

Jesus shared with the disciples in John 14 that He was going away to prepare a place for them but that He would come again to receive them. That promise also includes us. He goes on to profess Himself as the way, the truth and the life. In verse 16, He tells them, "And I will ask the Father, and he will give you another Counselor to be with you forever." Jesus was letting the disciples know then, and us now, that even though He was discontinuing His earthly ministry and was about to ascend to heaven with the Father, He was not leaving us alone. He was sending us a comforter, the Holy Spirit, who would be with us. Not only would He be *with* us, but He would also be *in* us (John 14:17–20).

The Holy Spirit Is Your Teacher

It is through the Holy Spirit that you come into the knowledge, understanding and ability to recall the Word of God. John 14:26 says, "But the Counselor, the Holy Spirit, whom the Father will send in my name, will teach you all things and will remind you of everything I have said to you." Luke 12:12, 1 Corinthians 2:13, and 1 John 2:27 are other Scriptures that reference the Holy Spirit as our teacher. When you accepted Christ, it was the Holy Spirit who pricked your heart, brought understanding, gave you a saving knowledge and brought you out of darkness into the marvelous light. You did not come to accept the saving power of Jesus Christ on your own. Understanding of the Word of God does not come to you by your own intellect. As you become closer to God, He reveals more of Himself to you through His Word. In other words, as you seek God each day, and grow closer to Him by studying His Word, He reveals more of Himself to you. You begin to understand the Word more than you did before. This is the Holy Spirit as teacher at work.

The Holy Spirit Intercedes

The Holy Spirit is your intercessor. He prays to the Father on your behalf when you are hurting and don't know what or how to pray. You can probably attest that you have been at a place in your life when you either could not pray or did not know how to pray. It is good news to know that when you can't or don't know how to pray, the Holy Spirit intercedes for you. Romans 8:26–27 says, "In the same way, the Spirit helps us in our weakness. We do not know what we ought to pray for, but the Spirit himself intercedes for us with groans that words cannot express. And he who searches our hearts knows the mind of the Spirit, because the Spirit intercedes for the saints in accordance with God's will." Praise God!

The Holy Spirit Convicts You of Sin

The Holy Spirit brings conviction of sin. John 16:8 tells us that the Holy Spirit reproves the world of sin, righteousness, and judgment. "In regard to sin, because men do not believe in me; in regard to righteousness, because I am going to the Father, where you can see me no longer; and in regard to judgment, because the prince of this world now stands condemned" (John 16: 9–11). For believers, the Holy Spirit pricks the conscience of sin. The little voice you hear that tells you when you should or should not do something or the feeling of despair that invades you when you have disobeyed God's Word, is the Holy Spirit at work. Psalm 38:18 says, "I confess my iniquity; I am troubled by my sin." If a child of God is able to sin and not feel convicted, something is wrong. When the Holy Spirit dwells within you, you will always feel a sense of unrest when you have disobeyed God. The good news is that God says, "If we confess our sins, he is faithful and just and will forgive us our sins and purify us from all unrighteousness" (1 John 1:9). Once you confess your sins to God, you are forgiven. You must know, if you feel guilt or shame after you have confessed, it is no longer the Holy Spirit, but Satan working as a liar, accuser, and deceiver. Remember, when you have confessed your sin, you are forgiven. God wipes the slate clean!

The Holy Spirit Seals You

After you hear the Word of God, receive the truth, and accept Christ as personal Savior, you are sealed by the Holy Spirit. "And you also were included in Christ when you heard the word of truth, the gospel of salvation. Having believed, you were marked in him with a seal, the promised Holy Spirit" (Ephesians 1:13). Salvation gives you security and protection. You are secure in the hands of the Father and protected from Satan. Romans 8:38–39 gives you security, "For I am convinced that neither death nor life, neither angels nor demons, neither the present nor the future, nor any powers, neither height nor depth, nor anything else in all creation, will be able to separate us from the love of God that is in Christ Jesus our Lord." You find protection in Luke 10:19, "I have given you authority to trample on snakes and scorpions and to overcome all the power of the enemy; nothing will harm you." Isn't it good news to know that whatever you may face in this life, you have security and protection because you are sealed by the Holy Spirit?

The Holy Spirit Works in the Church

The Holy Spirit not only works in the world reproving it of sin, but He is also at work in the church. He dwells within the people, who are themselves the temple. Ephesians 2:22 says, "And in him you too are being built together to become a dwelling in which God lives by his Spirit." The Spirit of God does not dwell within the church walls, but He is in midst of believers personally. Your body is the dwelling place of the Spirit. First Corinthians 6:19 reminds you that your body is the temple of the Holy Spirit which is in you. He also gives you gifts ". . . to prepare God's people for works of service, so that the body of Christ may be built up" (Ephesians 4:12). We will talk more about the gifts of the Spirit later.

The Holy Spirit Guides You into all Truth

The Holy Spirit will not allow you to be misled, but He gives you discernment and guidance into all truth. He removes the scales from your eyes and reveals truth and exposes deception. "But when he, the Spirit of truth, comes, he will guide you into all truth. He will not speak on his own; he will speak only what he hears, and he will tell you what is yet to come" (John 16:13).

THE GIFTS OF THE SPIRIT

Every child of God has been entrusted with at least one gift. Some have more than one, but every believer has at least one. Paul discusses the gifts of the Spirit in 1 Corinthians 12, Ephesians 4, and Romans 12. Some of the gifts mentioned include wisdom, knowledge, faith, healing, miracles, prophecy, discernment, tongues, interpretation of tongues, apostles, evangelists, pastors, teaching, exhortation, service, and mercy. God gives these gifts to His children so that His work can be done through them. Every gift is given for the glory of God and for the edification of the Saints. God wants to use you to bring others into the kingdom. The body of Christ (the church) is strengthened and unified as believers come together and utilize the gifts God has given them. The gifts are more than a talent because they are motivated and facilitated by the Holy Spirit. The Spirit within the person with the gift, reaches the Spirit within others, and as a result, lives are touched, saved, and transformed. This cannot be accomplished through talent.

God desires for each of His children to know and utilize their gifts to their fullest potential. What if you gave a friend a beautiful crystal bowl to be used as a unique centerpiece for the finest table in the house and later when you went over for a visit, you discovered the bowl sitting on a card table being used as an ashtray? You probably would feel extremely disappointed and hurt. Imagine how God feels when He gives His children gifts and they don't utilize them in the kingdom or don't use them to their fullest potential. When you refuse to use your spiritual gift(s), it paralyzes the body of Christ because that area of the body (the church) is not functioning.

There are several spiritual gift inventories available at your local Christian bookstore. I would encourage you to complete one and discuss it as a part of this lesson. You will find a list in the recommended resources section of the book. Pray and ask God for direction and revelation. He will confirm your spiritual gift to you. Make a commitment to God to utilize it to the best of your ability for His glory, and for the edification of the saints, whether it is in your home, at your job, or in the church.

THE FRUIT OF THE HOLY SPIRIT

"But the fruit of the Spirit is love, joy, peace, patience, kindness, goodness, faithfulness, gentleness and self-control. Against such things there is no law" (Galatians 5:22–23). The fruit of the Spirit is the proof in the pudding. The Bible says that you should bring forth fruit unto God (Romans 7:4). It is the fruit that bears witness to the life of the believer. Unlike the gifts of the Spirit, the fruit of the Spirit cannot be imitated. A person can pretend to love, have joy, peace and faith, be longsuffering, gentle, good, meek and temperate for only a short while. Eventually, the truth will come out. The fruit of the Spirit is the believer's evidence that Christ dwells within her. It is also a testament of *how much* Christ dwells within her. Your Christian walk involves making a conscious choice to walk in the Spirit and not fulfill the lust of the flesh (Galatians 5:16). Every day you should pray to be Spirit led in your conduct, your conversation, and your character.

Our Inward Struggle

Every Christian has an inward struggle with sin. Paul shared his struggle when he said, "When I want to do good, evil is right there with me" (Romans 7:21). There is a constant battle between the old nature and the new nature. We are reminded of the spiritual battle all Christians face in Ephesians 6:12, "For our struggle is not against flesh and blood, but against the rulers, against the authorities, against the powers of this dark world and against the spiritual forces of evil in the heavenly realms" (review Lesson 5 on spiritual warfare). As long as we were in darkness there was no struggle, but when we heard the truth of God's Word, it exposed the sin in our hearts. Romans 7:7–8 explains, "What shall we say, then? Is the law sin? Certainly not! Indeed I would not have known what sin was except through the law. For I would not have known what coveting really was if the law had not said, 'Do not covet.' But sin, seizing the opportunity afforded by the commandment, produced in me every kind of covetous desire. For apart from law, sin is dead." Paul was saying before he heard the Word of God he didn't know covetousness was sin, but after hearing the law God brought sin to light, creating a struggle within.

How do we handle this struggle? We must deny self (Matthew 16:24). Everyday we must consciously make the choice to choose Jesus and be led by the Spirit. There is no such thing as, "I couldn't help it" or "The devil made me do it." We can help it and the devil cannot *make* us do anything. He can only do what we *allow* him to do. Our walk with God is about choices. We must make the choice to crucify the flesh, recognizing that we cannot do it on our own. The Holy Spirit will empower us to conquer sin, making us victorious through Him. Romans 8:1 (KJV) says "There is therefore now no condemnation to them which are in Christ Jesus, who walk not after the flesh, but after the Spirit."

THE FREEDOM IN THE HOLY SPIRIT

"Then you will know the truth, and the truth will set you free" (John 8:32). Before receiving Christ, we were in bondage. We were servants to sin (John 3:34). Christ justified and freed us through His death, burial, and resurrection. After becoming saved, we can still be in bondage in our *condition*, if we are not aware of the freedom we have through our newly established *position* in Christ. "Therefore, if anyone is in Christ, he is a new creation; the old has gone, the new has come" (2 Corinthians 5:17). It is the Holy Spirit who empowers us to live a godly life. Galatians 5:17–18 says ". . . the sinful nature desires what is contrary to the Spirit, and the Spirit what is contrary to the sinful nature. They are in conflict with each other, so that you do not do what you want. But if you are led by the Spirit, you are not under law." The Holy Spirit makes us free from the law so we are no longer bound by sin. He gives us freedom from the bondage of the flesh so we can live holy lives. He also gives us freedom to fulfill His purpose so we can accomplish great things for the kingdom.

There is so much that can be taught about the person of the Holy Spirit. I don't believe it is possible to communicate all that He does. However, you must understand the Holy Spirit is not an *it*, but as the third person of the Godhead, He is alive in every person who professes Jesus as Lord. It is not the Holy Spirit who makes a person shout; your shouting should be the result of a conscious decision to worship God. The Holy Spirit does not dwell only within a particular group of Christians, but the Holy Spirit lives within every believer, working in their lives, empowering them daily to be *VICTORIOUS DISCIPLES!*

DISCUSSION QUESTIONS

1) What misconceptions have you had about the person of the Holy Spirit?

_____

_____

_____

_____

_____

_____

2) As we discussed the filling of the Holy Spirit, we addressed how the Holy Spirit comforts you, teaches you, intercedes for you, convicts you, seals you, works within the church, and guides you into all truth. Can you think of something else the Holy Spirit does for you?

_____

_____

_____

_____

_____

_____

3) What is your spiritual gift(s)? If you are not aware, there are various spiritual gift inventories available (see Appendix D). Discuss the results. Were you enlightened about your gift(s) or was the inventory confirmation of what you already knew?

_____

_____

_____

_____

_____

_____

4) Is the fruit of the Spirit evident in your life? Why? Why not?

_____

_____

_____

_____

_____

5) How do you handle the inward struggle with sin all Christians face?

_____

_____

_____

_____

_____

6) As a believer, you are free from the bondage of sin and the law. Is there an area in your life in which you are bound? Is there unconfessed sin in your life? Are you holding on to unforgiveness, jealousy, selfishness, pride, or any other sin? Are you willing to give it to God? (You may want to review the forgiveness section in Lesson 6).

_____

_____

_____

_____

_____

7) Do you now feel empowered to be a victorious disciple?

_____

_____

_____

_____

_____

LESSON 9 – EMPLOYED BY THE HOLY SPIRIT

Goal: To make the choice to allow the Holy Spirit to operate freely in your life

Homework Assignment:

- Review the lesson and identify how the Holy Spirit works in your life.

- Make a list and confess areas in your life in which you have not been led of the Spirit.

- Make a conscious choice everyday, every moment to live an obedient life by being led of the Spirit.

- Journal and share with the group next time.

_____

_____

_____

_____

_____

_____

_____

_____

_____

_____

_____

_____

_____

_____

Becoming a Disciple Leader

Therefore go and make disciples of all nations, baptizing them in the name of the Father and of the Son and of the Holy Spirit, and teaching them to obey everything I have commanded you. And surely I am with you always, to the very end of the age (Matthew 28:19–20).

Go and Make Disciples

As you complete this phase of Victorious Disciples, I pray that through your commitment to study and apply God's Word you have grown spiritually. Perhaps you have identified your spiritual gift(s) and God has given you a clearer picture of what He desires for you to do. Prayerfully, you have learned the importance of facing life's challenges through faith and you now realize you must trust God in areas of your life that you previously held on to. Perhaps you have worked through some dark areas in your life of unforgiveness, shame, guilt, doubt, fear, distrust, anxiety, hurt, and pain. You have allowed God to do a great work on the inside of you and you are now walking in victory. The journey may not have been easy and you must also be aware that life's challenges and difficulties will always be a part of the Christian journey. But now you have the faith and the knowledge that you are a victorious disciple and ". . . no weapon forged against you will prevail, and you will refute every tongue that accuses you" (Isaiah 54:17). Praise the Lord!

Be mindful that your journey does not stop here. You must continue to grow and strive to be transformed in Christ. To be Christ-like is to allow your life to reflect more of Christ and less of yourself daily. This involves self-denial, sacrifice, and obedience. Spiritual growth is a continuous process. It doesn't stop here. You, and you alone are responsible for your spiritual well being. It is not the responsibility of your pastor, spiritual leader, or mentor. You must see to it that you remain in God's Word, spend time in prayer, and continuously feed your spirit. I cannot stress this enough. You must daily study the Word of God. Not only do you have the responsibility of your own spiritual growth, but you are also given the responsibility to help others grow. The Christian walk must be intentional. It is not by chance that your life will be transformed or that you will bring others to Christ or encourage others in their walk. You must purpose to walk by faith. You must purpose to grow. You must make an effort to disciple others. Plants do not grow on their own. They must be watered and nurtured. As a Christian, you must see the need to nurture and pour into the lives of others.

You are instructed in the great commission to "go and make disciples of all nations, baptizing them in the name of the Father and of the Son and of the Holy Spirit, and teaching them to obey everything I have commanded you" (Matthew 28:19–20). The word "go" once again lets you know you must be intentional. You must be active and assertive. You cannot afford to be passive on this journey. There are too many lives that need to be saved and transformed. The Bible says to ". . . teach them" (Matthew 28:20). In other words, you must instruct them in the Word of God. The Bible also says, ". . . teach what I have commanded you", which means you should share what you know. God has not touched your life for you to keep it to yourself. You have the responsibility to share it with someone else. Not only do you have the *responsibility*, but you also have the *assurance* that He will be with you. He gives you the promise of His presence at the end of Matthew 28:20. "And surely I am with you always, to the very end of the age."

BE MY WITNESS

But you will receive power when the Holy Spirit comes on you; and you will be my witnesses in Jerusalem, and in all Judea and Samaria, and to the ends of the earth (Acts 1:8).

Not only is He *with* you, but He's also *in* you. "But you will receive power when the Holy Spirit comes on you; and you will be my witnesses in Jerusalem, and in all Judea and Samaria, and to the ends of the earth" (Acts 1:8). You are equipped through the Holy Spirit to go. At times you may feel inadequate to disciple others, but you must remember those whom God calls, He also equips. He will empower you to do that which He has called you to do.

Perhaps this year (or past months/weeks) God has placed a desire within you to disciple others. This is one of the goals of Victorious Disciples—to encourage women to disciple others. Victorious Disciples is a multiplying ministry. *If everyone disciples one, then everyone will be discipled!* This is not to say that everyone has a passion for discipleship. However, all Christians are commissioned to disciple. Does that mean you must lead a discipleship group? No. Just because you may not feel led to lead a discipleship group does not mean you are not a disciple leader. Every day you have the opportunity to share a word of encouragement with someone, to speak words of life to someone, to share a Scripture with someone who may be going through a difficult time. The life you live is your witness. Once again in Acts 1:8 Jesus says, after you have received the power of the Holy Spirit, you will "*be* my witness." Notice He did not say, "You will witness." In other words, your witness will be reflected in your life. It will be a part of your character and who you are as a person. It will not just be something that you profess with your mouth, but it will be something that you demonstrate in your daily living. As a result, people will be drawn to you and will seek your guidance. When they do, you will have a word from God for them and for their situation. Do not feel pressured in any way to go out tomorrow and begin a Victorious Disciples group. This may not be a good time for you for various reasons. Perhaps it will come later. But, always keep in mind that whether you lead a structured group or not, you are still a disciple leader. In addition, I recommend you focus on continuing your spiritual growth through the study of the Word and utilizing your spiritual gifts in your local church.

For those who feel led to begin a Victorious Disciples group, I would like to address a few things I believe are important for every leader to understand.

A Few Things to Consider Before Starting a Victorious Disciples Group

1) A disciple leader is always a teacher, but a teacher is not always a disciple leader

A disciple leader is one who teaches the Word of God, both by verbal impartation and by example. A teacher also teaches the Word of God by verbal impartation and example. What is the difference you might ask? The difference is the disciple leader's focus is not only teaching the Word, but also helping others to walk in the Word. The disciple leader should have a passion for helping individuals take the next step in their Christian walk—that is, moving from having knowledge of the Word, to applying it to their lives. The disciple leader helps people learn what faith looks like in their everyday life. It is one thing to know the Word, but it is another to live it. The disciple leader encourages, listens, motivates, gives insight, nurtures, instructs, holds others accountable, and even corrects when necessary. I call this *pouring into the lives of others,* and all this is done in the love of Jesus Christ.

I will never forget the first session of the first group I discipled. The session was so powerful. I could see on their faces how they were soaking up every word. They were hungry for God's Word and they came ready to receive what God had placed on my heart for them. When they left I was so full because I was reminded of how the disciples sat at Jesus' feet to be taught. That is what discipleship is—teaching, sharing, and walking with those whom God has placed in your circle of influence.

2) Your disciple group should begin with prayer

How should I select a group? Or should I choose the group? These are good questions. Every disciple leader should begin with prayer. Ask God to show you who He wants you to disciple. I promise if you pray this prayer, God will show you. He will place individuals in your path who need just what God has given you to share. Every individual I have ever discipled, shared the same response; "This is just what I needed." God will place people on your mind who are ready to go to the next level in their commitment to God. I believe this is a requirement to be discipled. The individual must want to grow. Keep in mind that everybody is not ready to be discipled and everyone will not want to be discipled. Some people are satisfied living a life of mediocrity in their Christian walk. But if you find individuals who want more in their walk with the Lord, and have a desire to grow, they will also have a desire to be discipled.

3) How do I approach someone who God has put on my heart?

Usually, the door to disciple someone will open for you. It may come through a conversation, a prayer request, or you may be asked. When God puts someone on my heart, I usually share with them about Victorious Disciples and tell them God placed them on my heart. I tell them to take some time to pray about their decision because they need to understand it is a commitment. They must be willing to make the sacrifice to attend the group study sessions and commit themselves to growing in their spiritual walk. It is a commitment to the Lord first and to the group second.

A Few Things to Consider After You Have Started a Victorious Disciples Group

1) Pray for Your Group Members

Not only should you pray for the group members prior to starting a group, but you should also pray for each individual of the group after you begin the group. You should pray for the group collectively and individually. The members need to know you are concerned enough about them to go to the Father on their behalf.

2) Identify Their Spiritual Gifts

As you get to know your group members through studying, sharing, fellowshipping, and praying together, God may give you insight and discernment about their strengths, abilities, and spiritual gifts. You will want to share this with each one. Ask God for guidance as to whether it is something that should be shared within the group or privately. When you see them do well in a particular area, point that out. Your words of affirmation will have a lasting affect. It makes a great impact on one's life to have what they may feel God is doing in their heart confirmed by another believer. For some it may be a surprise. They may not realize their area of giftedness. For others it may be confirmation, which will bring them great joy to know that others see growth and maturity in their walk.

3) Be Available

As a disciple leader, you are making a commitment as well. Your commitment is not just for the two-hour Bible study once a week or month, but your commitment is twenty-four hours a day, seven days a week. This is not to say there should be no boundaries, but I think you get my point. There may be times when you are called upon at a time other than your group study time. Within reason, you should make yourself available. This means you must be willing to be somewhat accessible to your group members. They need to know if they need to talk to you, they have your permission to call you and you will take the time to talk to them.

4) Lead Them to God—Not Dependency

Some group members may talk with their group leader about personal experiences. They may share some painful experiences or perhaps some things they have never shared with anyone else. The possibility for a group member to become dependent upon the group leader can be great if the group leader is not careful to direct the individual to God. Yes, you should be there for them to encourage them, to listen to them and to help them through. But most of all, you should be there to pray with them and instruct them according to the Word of God concerning their situation. The goal of Victorious Disciples is spiritual growth, not spiritual dependency. It is not healthy for a leader to need or desire group members to need them for every problem that should arise in their lives. Nor is it healthy for group members to feel the need to call on their group leader for every minor problem. You may find some group members may call you for help more frequently, however, your task is always to lead them to Jesus. If you find yourself in a situation where an individual is having serious problems on a long-term basis, or you feel unequipped to handle what they are bringing to you, you might refer them to a Christian counselor.

5) Practice Confidentiality

Keep everything group members share with you in confidence—in confidence. Information about group members should not be shared with anyone. You should not discuss one group member with another group member. Information shared with you should not be discussed within the group unless the individual brings it up or they have given you permission to discuss it. Nothing can hurt more or do more damage to a person than to have their trust betrayed by someone they trust. It is difficult to restore a breach of trust. Confidentiality should also be addressed with the whole group. Group members must understand they are expected to regard the confidence of each group member. However, it should be understood that in the case of threat of hurt, harm or danger to oneself or others, confidentiality is disregarded. Professional counselors are obligated to disregard confidentiality boundaries in the case of a life-threatening emergency. I believe this is a good practice for any individual. It should be understood within the group that in such a case, proper authorities will be notified for their protection.

6) Be a Person of Your Word

People will only trust you when you have proved that they can. Be a person of your word and do what you say you will do. Be consistent with your meeting times. If you find that you have to reschedule, let them know in advance. Be on time for your group sessions. Be prepared. Return their phone calls. If you are a person of your word, they will be too.

7) Understand Group Dynamics

As much as we would like to think there are no problems or disagreements within disciple groups, this may not always be the case. People are human and sometimes problems arise. As a result, it is important to have some basic understanding of group dynamics. Every group will be different because the people who make up the group are different. Some groups will run smoothly and others may experience some bumps here and there. Conflict can arise, and when it does, it should be handled in love. As the disciple leader, you should always set the example. One rule of thumb I usually follow: If a group member approaches me with concerns regarding the group, I encourage them to address it within the group. I then serve as a mediator to help the group come to an understanding. If two individuals are having problems within the group, once again, I encourage them to work it out among themselves and if necessary, as leader, I help them work it out. Do not allow disagreements to linger. This only opens the door for Satan to bring division within the group. A part of growing in Christ is learning how to deal with conflict in a way that pleases God. Ephesians 4:26 says "In your anger do not sin: Do not let the sun go down while you are still angry." Helping individuals deal with conflict within the group will help them learn how to resolve conflict in their personal lives.

8) Respect the Individuality of Each Group Member

As a disciple leader, you will find that each member of the group may be at different spiritual levels. This is to be expected and you will need to meet each individual where they are. This means some individuals may need more than others. They may require more one-on-one time. They may need more encouragement, counseling, listening, and time in general. It is crucial that you do not become frustrated because they are not at the same level as others in the group. You may even find some to be rebellious. Keep in mind that not everyone really wants to be discipled. Becoming a disciple means making the commitment to move from having head knowledge of the Word of God to living it. It takes a mature Christian to make the decision to make that step. Don't give up on them. Be loving, gentle, and patient.

9) Take Care of Yourself

You cannot pour into the lives of others if your life is empty. That means you must take care of your own spiritual needs first. Make sure you are consistently spending time with the Lord. In addition to getting your personal spiritual nourishment, try to have your own spiritual mentor who can share with you, pray with you, and encourage you. You too need someone to speak life into you or else you will find yourself running on fumes, frustrated and unable to give to others.

A FEW THINGS TO CONSIDER AFTER YOUR DISCIPLE GROUP ENDS

The disciple leader should be led of the Lord. It is a commitment that requires love, patience, giving, time, and much prayer. The disciple leader must love God and live a life that adheres to His Word. It has been said, "The only Bible some people may read is the life you live." As a disciple leader it is important that your walk falls in line with your talk. Nothing can be more hurtful and discrediting to your ministry than to live a life that is contrary to what you teach. This does not mean that you will be perfect. It does mean you are striving daily to be led of the Spirit in all you say and do. People will be drawn to your sincerity and genuine heart.

Prayerfully, when one group ends, God will place others on your heart and you will continue the multiplying ministry of discipleship. Perhaps the members of your group will be led to begin their own groups. If that is the case, you might consider following up with them on a regular basis to provide ongoing encouragement. As leaders are developed in your church or area, you should establish a quarterly group session for leaders, to provide additional encouragement and support. You may obtain more information on quarterly leader's groups at the end of the book on the *Contact Us* form or look for the upcoming leader's manual to be published in the summer of 2004.

As you consider becoming a disciple leader, Jesus is your example. Your relationship with those you disciple should mirror that of Jesus and His disciples. As you examine Jesus' life, you see His love for the disciples. He spent time with them. He taught them. He was an example for them. He encouraged them and He pointed them to the Father. This is the model you should follow as you make the commitment to *pour into the lives of others*. **Remember, if everyone disciples one, then everyone will be discipled!**

LESSON 10 – BECOMING A DISCIPLE LEADER

Goals: To help you assess your readiness to become a disciple leader, to help you determine whether God is leading you to become a disciple leader directly (over a structured group) or indirectly (through your daily interactions with people), and to provide some things to consider before leading a group.

Homework Assignment:

- Commit to prayer the decision to become a disciple leader.

- Listen for God's voice and determine if He is telling you to:
    - Continue to grow spiritually through the study of God's Word
    - Join in God's kingdom work in the area of your spiritual gifts on your job, in your church or in your community.
    - Pour into the lives of others through leading a Victorious Disciples group

- If you are unsure, seek the counsel of your disciple leader.

_____

_____

_____

_____

_____

_____

_____

_____

_____

_____

Reflections and Growth Assessment

But as for you, continue in what you have learned and have become convinced of, because you know those from whom you learned it (2 Timothy 3:14).

*N*ow that you have completed the Victorious Disciples study, take a few moments to reflect upon your spiritual growth during the past several months/weeks. Answer these questions and discuss them within your group.

1) Introduction

Look at the Needs Assessment/Commitment form you completed at the beginning of Victorious Disciples. Did you meet your goals?

_____

_____

_____

_____

_____

2) Lesson 1—Knowing Who You Are in Christ

Do you have a better understanding of who you are in Christ? How has this knowledge impacted your life? Review your spiritual gift inventory. Discuss your spiritual gift(s). Are you utilizing it/them? Are you fulfilling God's purpose for your life? What is God calling you to do and how can you move towards doing it? Review your personal mission statement. How has it impacted your life?

_____

_____

_____

_____

_____

3) Lesson 2—How to Study the Bible

Has your personal Bible study changed this year? In what way? What can you do to improve your knowledge of the Word of God?

_____

_____

_____

_____

_____

4) Lesson 3—The Journey of Faith

Think about how you handled adversity in your life one year ago. Has there been any change? In what ways have you seen your faith increase?

_____

_____

_____

_____

5) Lesson 4—Becoming a Woman of Prayer

How has your prayer life changed this year? Are you praying more or less? Review your prayer journal. What prayers has God answered for you this year? Did He answer in a way you expected or differently?

_____

_____

_____

_____

_____

6) Lesson 5—How to Fight the Battle and Win

In what ways have you experienced spiritual warfare? Were you able to identify the work of Satan? How did you respond? How was your response different than before? How has the use of Scripture impacted the battle?

_____

_____

_____

_____

_____

7) Lesson 6—Love That Forgives

What changes have you seen in your life as it relates to love and forgiveness? Have any of your relationships changed this year? In what way?

_____

_____

_____

_____

_____

8) Lesson 7—Fasting for a Breakthrough

Discuss your experience of fasting. How did it affect your life spiritually?

_____

_____

_____

_____

_____

9) Lesson 8—Created for Worship

Describe how your personal and corporate worship has changed.

_____

_____

_____

_____

_____

10) Lesson 9—Empowered by the Holy Spirit

Has your understanding of the Holy Spirit changed? Explain. How do you see the Holy Spirit working in your life?

_____

_____

_____

_____

_____

11) Lesson 10—Becoming a Disciple Leader

Do you feel led to become a disciple leader? Why/Why not?

_____

_____

_____

_____

_____

PERSONAL EVALUATION

12) In what specific areas in your life have you seen growth as a result of Victorious Disciples?

_____

_____

_____

_____

_____

_____

13) List three specific areas in your life that you have discovered need continuous growth.

_____

_____

_____

_____

_____

_____

14) As stated previously (Lesson 10), your spiritual growth is your responsibility. It does not stop here. What is your plan to ensure your continued spiritual growth? Be specific.

A) _____

B) _____

C) _____

D) _____

E) _____

15) How do you plan to take what you have learned and share it with others?

_____

_____

_____

_____

_____

_____

16) Write a paragraph on your spiritual journey for the past year (or months).

_____

_____

_____

_____

_____

Prayer Journal

Growth Journal

_____
_____
_____
_____
_____
_____
_____
_____
_____
_____
_____
_____
_____
_____
_____
_____

Growth Journal

Growth Journal

Scripture Journal

Scripture Journal

VICTORY VERSES

Encouragement for the Journey

Romans 8:37

No, in all these things we are more than conquerors through him who loved us.

Philippians 4:13

I can do everything through him who gives me strength.

Philippians 4: 6–7

Do not be anxious about anything, but in everything, by prayer and petition, with thanksgiving, present your requests to God. And the peace of God, which transcends all understanding, will guard your hearts and your minds in Christ Jesus.

Philippians 4:19

And my God will meet all your needs according to his glorious riches in Christ Jesus.

Romans 8:28

And we know that in all things God works for the good of those who love him, who have been called according to his purpose.

Isaiah 26:3

You will keep in perfect peace him whose mind is steadfast, because he trusts in you.

Matthew 6:25–34

Therefore I tell you, do not worry about your life, what you will eat or drink; or about your body, what you will wear. Is not life more important than food, and the body more important than clothes? Look at the birds of the air; they do not sow or reap or store away in barns, and yet your heavenly Father feeds them. Are you not much more valuable than they? Who of you by worrying can add a single hour to his life? And why do you worry about clothes? See how the lilies of the field grow. They do not labor or spin. Yet I tell you that not even Solomon in all his splendor was dressed like one of these. If that is how God clothes the grass of the field, which is here today and tomorrow is thrown into the fire, will he not much more clothe you, O you of little faith? So do not worry, saying, 'What shall we eat?' or 'What shall we drink?' or 'What shall we wear?' For the pagans run after all these things, and your heavenly Father knows that you need them. But seek first his kingdom and his righteousness, and all these things will be given to you as well. Therefore do not worry about tomorrow, for tomorrow will worry about itself. Each day has enough trouble of its own.

Proverbs 3:24

When you lie down, you will not be afraid; when you lie down, your sleep will be sweet.

Psalm 119:165

Great peace have they who love your law, and nothing can make them stumble.

John 14:27

Peace I leave with you; my peace I give you. I do not give to you as the world gives. Do not let your hearts be troubled and do not be afraid.

Psalm 23:4

Even though I walk through the valley of the shadow of death, I will fear no evil, for you are with me; your rod and your staff, they comfort me.

2 Timothy 1:7

For God did not give us a spirit of timidity, but a spirit of power, of love and of self-discipline.

Psalm 55:22

Cast your cares on the LORD and he will sustain you; he will never let the righteous fall.

Psalm 32:8

I will instruct you and teach you in the way you should go; I will counsel you and watch over you.

Proverbs 3:5–6

Trust in the LORD with all your heart and lean not on your own understanding; in all your ways acknowledge him, and he will make your paths straight.

SPIRITUAL WARFARE

Ephesians 6:12

For our struggle is not against flesh and blood, but against the rulers, against the authorities, against the powers of this dark world and against the spiritual forces of evil in the heavenly realms.

2 Corinthians 10:3–5

For though we live in the world, we do not wage war as the world does. The weapons we fight with are not the weapons of the world. On the contrary, they have divine power to demolish strongholds. We demolish arguments and every pretension that sets itself up against the knowledge of God, and we take captive every thought to make it obedient to Christ.

Revelation 12:11

They overcame him by the blood of the Lamb and by the word of their testimony; they did not love their lives so much as to shrink from death.

Ephesians 6:13–18

Therefore put on the full armor of God, so that when the day of evil comes, you may be able to stand your ground, and after you have done everything, to stand. Stand firm then, with the belt of truth buckled around your waist, with the breastplate of righteousness in place, and with your feet fitted with the readiness that comes from the gospel of peace. In addition to all this, take up the shield of faith, with which you can extinguish all the flaming arrows of the evil one. Take the helmet of salvation and the sword of the Spirit, which is the word of God. And pray in the Spirit on all occasions with all kinds of prayers and requests. With this in mind, be alert and always keep on praying for all the saints.

2 Chronicles 16:9

For the eyes of the LORD range throughout the earth to strengthen those whose hearts are fully committed to him.

Psalm 34:7

The angel of the LORD encamps around those who fear him, and he delivers them.

Psalm 91:4

He will cover you with his feathers, and under his wings you will find refuge; his faithfulness will be your shield and rampart.

Psalm 125:2

As the mountains surround Jerusalem, so the LORD surrounds his people both now and forevermore.

Exodus 14:14

The LORD will fight for you; you need only to be still.

2 Chronicles 20:15

Do not be afraid or discouraged because of this vast army. For the battle is not yours, but God's.

Isaiah 54:17

No weapon forged against you will prevail, and you will refute every tongue that accuses you. This is the heritage of the servants of the LORD, and this is their vindication from me," declares the LORD.

Matthew 18:18

I tell you the truth, whatever you bind on earth will be bound in heaven, and whatever you loose on earth will be loosed in heaven.

Philippians 4:8

Finally, brothers, whatever is true, whatever is noble, whatever is right, whatever is pure, whatever is lovely, whatever is admirable—if anything is excellent or praiseworthy—think about such things.

Recommended Resources

Anderson, Neil T. *The Bondage Breaker*. Eugene, Oregon: Harvest House, 1993.

Arthur, Kay. *How to Study the Bible*. Eugene, Oregon: Harvest House, 1994.

Banner of Truth. Robert Murray M'Cheyne's Calendar for Daily Bible Readings. To order copies of the book call toll free 1-800-263-8025.

Biblical Personal Profile System. Minneapolis: Inscape Publishing, 1995.

Blackaby, Henry T., and Claude V King. *Experiencing God*. Nashville: Broadman & Holman, 1994.

Cook, Dr. S. Johnson. *Too Blessed to be Stressed*. Nashville: Thomas Nelson Publisher, 1998.

Copeland, Germaine. *Prayers that Avail Much*. Tulsa, Oklahoma: Harrison House, 1987.

Cymbala, Jim. *Fresh Faith*. Grand Rapids, Michigan: Zondervan Publishing House, 1999.

Cymbala, Jim. *Fresh Wind, Fresh Fire*. Grand Rapids, Michigan: Zondervan Publishing House, 1997.

Davis, Denny D. *Understanding Spiritual Gifts*. Cassette tape. *http://www.sjbcfamily.com*.

Davis, Denny D. *Manifesting the fruit of the Spirit*. Cassette tape. *http://www.sjbcfamily.com*.

Evans, Tony. *The Battle is the Lord's*. Chicago: Moody, 1998.

Evans, Tony. *The Perfect Christian*. Nashville: Word Publishing, 1998.

Foster, Richard J. *Celebration of Discipline*. New York: HarperCollins, 1998.

Frangipane, Francis. *The Three Battlegrounds*. Cedar Rapids, Iowa: Arrow Publications, 1989.

George, Elizabeth. *A Woman After God's own Heart*. Eugene, Oregon: Harvest House, 1997.

Gilbert, Larry. *Spiritual Gifts Inventory*. Oxnard, California: Church Growth Institute, 1995.

Jeffrey, Arnold. *Discovering the Bible for Yourself*. Downers Grove, Illinois: Intervarsity Press, 1993.

MacDonald, Gordon. *Ordering Your Private World*. Nashville: Thomas Nelson Publisher, 1985.

Meyers, Joyce. *Me and My Big Mouth*. Tulsa, Oklahoma: Harrison House, 1997.

Meyers, Joyce. *Battlefield of the Mind*. Tulsa, Oklahoma: Harrison House, 1995.

Strong, James. *The New Strong's Exhaustive Concordance of the Bible*. Nashville: Thomas Nelson Publishers, 1995.

Tenney, Tommy. *The God Chasers*. Shippensburg, Pennsylvania: Destiny Image, 1998.

Thompson, Frank Charles, and G. Fredrick Owen. *Thompson Chain-Reference Bible*. Indianapolis, Indiana: B.B. Kirkbride Bible Company, Inc., 1988.

Vine, W.E., Merrill F. Unger, and William White Jr. *The Vine's Complete Expository Dictionary of Old and New Testament Words*: Thomas Nelson Publishers: Nashville, 1985.

Wagner, C. Peter. *Finding Your Spiritual Gifts—Wagner-Modified Houts Questionnaire*. Ventura, California: Gospel Light, 1995.

Wells, Thelma. *The Best Devotions of Thelma Wells*. Grand Rapids, Minnesota: Zondervan Publishing House, 2001.

Wesley, Karry D. *Hanging Tough in Tough Times*. Enumclaw, Washington: WinePress Publishing, 2000.

Wesley, Karry D. *The Study of the Gospel of Mark*. Enumclaw, Washington: WinePress Publishing, 1999.

Wilson, P.B. *Liberated Through Submission*. Eugene, Oregon: Harvest House, 1990.

APPENDIX E

Bibliography

Anderson, Neil T. *The Bondage Breaker*. Eugene, Oregon: Harvest House, 1993.

Anderson, Neil T. *The Steps to Freedom*. Ventura, California: Gospel Light, 1996.

Arthur, Kay. *How to Study the Bible*. Eugene, Oregon: Harvest House, 1994.

Barker, Kenneth. The NIV Study Bible. Grand Rapids, Minnesota: Zondervan Publishing House, 1995.

Blackaby, Henry T., and Claude V. King. *Experiencing God*. Nashville: Broadman & Holman Publishers, 1994.

Evans, Tony. *Get Serious: Daily Devotions to Keep You Close to God*. Wheaton, IL: Crossway Books, 1995.

Evans, Tony. *The Battle is the Lord's*. Chicago: Moody Press, 1998.

Floyd, Ronnie W. *The Power of Prayer and Fasting*. Nashville: Broadman & Holman, 1997.

Foster, Richard J. *Celebration of Discipline*. New York: HarperCollins, 1998.

Graham, Billy. *The Collected Works of Billy Graham*. New York: Inspirational Press, 1993.

Henry, Matthew. *Matthew Henry's Commentary on the Whole Bible*. Peabody, Massachusetts: Hendrickson Publishers 1991.

Hicks, H. Beecher, Jr. *Preaching Through a Storm*. Grand Rapids, Minnesota: Zondervan Publishing House, 1987.

Jeffrey, Arnold. *Discovering the Bible for Yourself*. Downers Grove, Illinois: Intervarsity Press, 1993.

Jeremiah, David. (Cassette tape) *What is Worship?*

Jeremiah, David. (Cassette tape) *The Importance of Worship.*

Tenney, Tommy. *The God Chasers*. Shippensburg, Pennsylvania: Destiny Image, 1998.

Thompson, Frank Charles, and G. Fredrick Owen. *Thompson Chain-Reference Bible*. Indianapolis, Indiana: B.B. Kirkbride Bible Company, Inc., 1988.

Torrey, R. A. *How to Study the Bible*. New Kensington, Pennsylvania: Whitaker House, 1985.

Towns, Elmer L. *Fasting for a Spiritual Breakthrough*. Ventura, California: Regal Books, 1996.

Wagner, C. Peter. *Your Spiritual Gifts Can Help Your Church Grow*. Ventura, California: Regal Books, 1994.

Wesley, Cheryl. Rivers of Grace Ministry Women's Conference, 1998.

January

This is my beloved Son, in whom I am well pleased; hear ye him.

Family				Date	Secret			
Book	**Chapter**	**Book**	**Chapter**		**Book**	**Chapter**	**Book**	**Chapter**
Genesis	1	Matthew	1	1	Ezra	1	Acts	1
Genesis	2	Matthew	2	2	Ezra	2	Acts	2
Genesis	3	Matthew	3	3	Ezra	3	Acts	3
Genesis	4	Matthew	4	4	Ezra	4	Acts	4
Genesis	5	Matthew	5	5	Ezra	5	Acts	5
Genesis	6	Matthew	6	6	Ezra	6	Acts	6
Genesis	7	Matthew	7	7	Ezra	7	Acts	7
Genesis	8	Matthew	8	8	Ezra	8	Acts	8
Genesis	9,10	Matthew	9	9	Ezra	9	Acts	9
Genesis	11	Matthew	10	10	Ezra	10	Acts	10
Genesis	12	Matthew	11	11	Nehemiah	1	Acts	11
Genesis	13	Matthew	12	12	Nehemiah	2	Acts	12
Genesis	14	Matthew	13	13	Nehemiah	3	Acts	13
Genesis	15	Matthew	14	14	Nehemiah	4	Acts	14
Genesis	16	Matthew	15	15	Nehemiah	5	Acts	15
Genesis	17	Matthew	16	16	Nehemiah	6	Acts	16
Genesis	18	Matthew	17	17	Nehemiah	7	Acts	17
Genesis	19	Matthew	18	18	Nehemiah	8	Acts	18
Genesis	20	Matthew	19	19	Nehemiah	9	Acts	19
Genesis	21	Matthew	20	20	Nehemiah	10	Acts	20
Genesis	22	Matthew	21	21	Nehemiah	11	Acts	21
Genesis	23	Matthew	22	22	Nehemiah	12	Acts	22
Genesis	24	Matthew	23	23	Nehemiah	13	Acts	23
Genesis	25	Matthew	24	24	Esther	1	Acts	24
Genesis	26	Matthew	25	25	Esther	2	Acts	25
Genesis	27	Matthew	26	26	Esther	3	Acts	26
Genesis	28	Matthew	27	27	Esther	4	Acts	27
Genesis	29	Matthew	28	28	Esther	5	Acts	28
Genesis	30	Mark	1	29	Esther	6	Romans	1
Genesis	31	Mark	2	30	Esther	7	Romans	2
Genesis	32	Mark	3	31	Esther	8	Romans	3

February

I have esteemed the words of his mouth more than my necessary food.

Family				Date	Secret			
Book	**Chapter**	**Book**	**Chapter**		**Book**	**Chapter**	**Book**	**Chapter**
Genesis	33	Mark	4	1	Esther	9,10	Romans	4
Genesis	34	Mark	5	2	Job	1	Romans	5
Genesis	35,36	Mark	6	3	Job	2	Romans	6
Genesis	37	Mark	7	4	Job	3	Romans	7
Genesis	38	Mark	8	5	Job	4	Romans	8
Genesis	39	Mark	9	6	Job	5	Romans	9
Genesis	40	Mark	10	7	Job	6	Romans	10
Genesis	41	Mark	11	8	Job	7	Romans	11
Genesis	42	Mark	12	9	Job	8	Romans	12
Genesis	43	Mark	13	10	Job	9	Romans	13
Genesis	44	Mark	14	11	Job	10	Romans	14
Genesis	45	Mark	15	12	Job	11	Romans	15
Genesis	46	Mark	16	13	Job	12	Romans	16
Genesis	47	Luke	1:1-38	14	Job	13	1 Corinthians	1
Genesis	48	Luke	1:39-80	15	Job	14	1 Corinthians	2
Genesis	49	Luke	2	16	Job	15	1 Corinthians	3
Genesis	50	Luke	3	17	Job	16,17	1 Corinthians	4
Exodus	1	Luke	4	18	Job	18	1 Corinthians	5
Exodus	2	Luke	5	19	Job	19	1 Corinthians	6
Exodus	3	Luke	6	20	Job	20	1 Corinthians	7
Exodus	4	Luke	7	21	Job	21	1 Corinthians	8
Exodus	5	Luke	8	22	Job	22	1 Corinthians	9
Exodus	6	Luke	9	23	Job	23	1 Corinthians	10
Exodus	7	Luke	10	24	Job	24	1 Corinthians	11
Exodus	8	Luke	11	25	Job	25,26	1 Corinthians	12
Exodus	9	Luke	12	26	Job	27	1 Corinthians	13
Exodus	10	Luke	13	27	Job	28	1 Corinthians	14
Exodus	11,12:1-21	Luke	14	28	Job	29	1 Corinthians	15

Reading Instructions:

The center column contains the day of the month. The two first columns contain the chapter to be read in the family. The two last columns contain the calendar portions to be read in secret.

Robert Murray M'Cheyne's Calendar for Daily Bible Readings

March

Mary kept all these things, and pondered them in her heart.

Family				Date	Secret			
Book	Chapter	Book	Chapter		Book	Chapter	Book	Chapter
Exodus	12:22-51	Luke	15	1	Job	30	1 Corinthians	16
Exodus	13	Luke	16	2	Job	31	2 Corinthians	1
Exodus	14	Luke	17	3	Job	32	2 Corinthians	2
Exodus	15	Luke	18	4	Job	33	2 Corinthians	3
Exodus	16	Luke	19	5	Job	34	2 Corinthians	4
Exodus	17	Luke	20	6	Job	35	2 Corinthians	5
Exodus	18	Luke	21	7	Job	36	2 Corinthians	6
Exodus	19	Luke	22	8	Job	37	2 Corinthians	7
Exodus	20	Luke	23	9	Job	38	2 Corinthians	8
Exodus	21	Luke	24	10	Job	39	2 Corinthians	9
Exodus	22	John	1	11	Job	40	2 Corinthians	10
Exodus	23	John	2	12	Job	41	2 Corinthians	11
Exodus	24	John	3	13	Job	42	2 Corinthians	12
Exodus	25	John	4	14	Proverbs	1	2 Corinthians	13
Exodus	26	John	5	15	Proverbs	2	Galatians	1
Exodus	27	John	6	16	Proverbs	3	Galatians	2
Exodus	28	John	7	17	Proverbs	4	Galatians	3
Exodus	29	John	8	18	Proverbs	5	Galatians	4
Exodus	30	John	9	19	Proverbs	6	Galatians	5
Exodus	31	John	10	20	Proverbs	7	Galatians	6
Exodus	32	John	11	21	Proverbs	8	Ephesians	1
Exodus	33	John	12	22	Proverbs	9	Ephesians	2
Exodus	34	John	13	23	Proverbs	10	Ephesians	3
Exodus	35	John	14	24	Proverbs	11	Ephesians	4
Exodus	36	John	15	25	Proverbs	12	Ephesians	5
Exodus	37	John	16	26	Proverbs	13	Ephesians	6
Exodus	38	John	17	27	Proverbs	14	Philippians	1
Exodus	39	John	18	28	Proverbs	15	Philippians	2
Exodus	40	John	19	29	Proverbs	16	Philippians	3
Leviticus	1	John	20	30	Proverbs	17	Philippians	4
Leviticus	2,3	John	21	31	Proverbs	18	Colossians	1

Robert Murray M'Cheyne's Calendar for Daily Bible Readings

April

O send out thy light and thy truth; let them lead me.

Family				Date	Secret			
Book	Chapter	Book	Chapter		Book	Chapter	Book	Chapter
Leviticus	4	Psalms	1,2	1	Proverbs	19	Colossians	2
Leviticus	5	Psalms	3,4	2	Proverbs	20	Colossians	3
Leviticus	6	Psalms	5,6	3	Proverbs	21	Colossians	4
Leviticus	7	Psalms	7,8	4	Proverbs	22	1 Thessalonians	1
Leviticus	8	Psalms	9	5	Proverbs	23	1 Thessalonians	2
Leviticus	9	Psalms	10	6	Proverbs	24	1 Thessalonians	3
Leviticus	10	Psalms	11,12	7	Proverbs	25	1 Thessalonians	4
Leviticus	11,12	Psalms	13,14	8	Proverbs	26	1 Thessalonians	5
Leviticus	13	Psalms	15,16	9	Proverbs	27	2 Thessalonians	1
Leviticus	14	Psalms	17	10	Proverbs	28	2 Thessalonians	2
Leviticus	15	Psalms	18	11	Proverbs	29	2 Thessalonians	3
Leviticus	16	Psalms	19	12	Proverbs	30	1 Timothy	1
Leviticus	17	Psalms	20,21	13	Proverbs	31	1 Timothy	2
Leviticus	18	Psalms	22	14	Ecclesiastes	1	1 Timothy	3
Leviticus	19	Psalms	23,24	15	Ecclesiastes	2	1 Timothy	4
Leviticus	20	Psalms	25	16	Ecclesiastes	3	1 Timothy	5
Leviticus	21	Psalms	26,27	17	Ecclesiastes	4	1 Timothy	6
Leviticus	22	Psalms	28,29	18	Ecclesiastes	5	2 Timothy	1
Leviticus	23	Psalms	30	19	Ecclesiastes	6	2 Timothy	2
Leviticus	24	Psalms	31	20	Ecclesiastes	7	2 Timothy	3
Leviticus	25	Psalms	32	21	Ecclesiastes	8	2 Timothy	4
Leviticus	26	Psalms	33	22	Ecclesiastes	9	Titus	1
Leviticus	27	Psalms	34	23	Ecclesiastes	10	Titus	2
Numbers	1	Psalms	35	24	Ecclesiastes	11	Titus	3
Numbers	2	Psalms	36	25	Ecclesiastes	12	Philemon	1
Numbers	3	Psalms	37	26	Song	1	Hebrews	1
Numbers	4	Psalms	38	27	Song	2	Hebrews	2
Numbers	5	Psalms	39	28	Song	3	Hebrews	3
Numbers	6	Psalms	40,41	29	Song	4	Hebrews	4
Numbers	7	Psalms	42,43	30	Song	5	Hebrews	5

Reading Instructions:

The center column contains the day of the month. The two first columns contain the cha
the family. The two last columns contain the portions to be read in secret.

May

From a child thou hast known the holy Scriptures

Book	Chapter	Book	Chapter	Date	Book	Chapter	Book	Chapter
Numbers	8	Psalms	44	1	Song	6	Hebrews	6
Numbers	9	Psalms	45	2	Song	7	Hebrews	7
Numbers	10	Psalms	46,47	3	Song	8	Hebrews	8
Numbers	11	Psalms	48	4	Isaiah	1	Hebrews	9
Numbers	12,13	Psalms	49	5	Isaiah	2	Hebrews	10
Numbers	14	Psalms	50	6	Isaiah	3,4	Hebrews	11
Numbers	15	Psalms	51	7	Isaiah	5	Hebrews	12
Numbers	16	Psalms	52,53,54	8	Isaiah	6	Hebrews	13
Numbers	17,18	Psalms	55	9	Isaiah	7	James	1
Numbers	19	Psalms	56,57	10	Isaiah	8,9:1-7	James	2
Numbers	20	Psalms	58,59	11	Isaiah	9:7-21,10:1-4	James	3
Numbers	21	Psalms	60,61	12	Isaiah	10:5-34	James	4
Numbers	22	Psalms	62,63	13	Isaiah	11,12	James	5
Numbers	23	Psalms	64,65	14	Isaiah	13	1 Peter	1
Numbers	24	Psalms	66,67	15	Isaiah	14	1 Peter	2
Numbers	25	Psalms	68	16	Isaiah	15	1 Peter	3
Numbers	26	Psalms	69	17	Isaiah	16	1 Peter	4
Numbers	27	Psalms	70,71	18	Isaiah	17,18	1 Peter	5
Numbers	28	Psalms	72	19	Isaiah	19,20	2 Peter	1
Numbers	29	Psalms	73	20	Isaiah	21	2 Peter	2
Numbers	30	Psalms	74	21	Isaiah	22	2 Peter	3
Numbers	31	Psalms	75,76	22	Isaiah	23	1 John	1
Numbers	32	Psalms	77	23	Isaiah	24	1 John	2
Numbers	33	Psalms	78:1-37	24	Isaiah	25	1 John	3
Numbers	34	Psalms	78:38-72	25	Isaiah	26	1 John	4
Numbers	35	Psalms	79	26	Isaiah	27	1 John	5
Numbers	36	Psalms	80	27	Isaiah	28	2 John	1
Deuteronomy	1	Psalms	81,82	28	Isaiah	29	3 John	1
Deuteronomy	2	Psalms	83,84	29	Isaiah	30	Jude	1
Deuteronomy	3	Psalms	85	30	Isaiah	31	Revelation	1
Deuteronomy	4	Psalms	86,87	31	Isaiah	32	Revelation	2

June

Blessed is he that readeth and they that hear.

Book	Chapter	Book	Chapter	Date	Book	Chapter	Book	Chapter
Deuteronomy	5	Psalms	88	1	Isaiah	33	Revelation	3
Deuteronomy	6	Psalms	89	2	Isaiah	34	Revelation	4
Deuteronomy	7	Psalms	90	3	Isaiah	35	Revelation	5
Deuteronomy	8	Psalms	91	4	Isaiah	36	Revelation	6
Deuteronomy	9	Psalms	92,93	5	Isaiah	37	Revelation	7
Deuteronomy	10	Psalms	94	6	Isaiah	38	Revelation	8
Deuteronomy	11	Psalms	95,96	7	Isaiah	39	Revelation	9
Deuteronomy	12	Psalms	97,98	8	Isaiah	40	Revelation	10
Deuteronomy	13,14	Psalms	99,100,101	9	Isaiah	41	Revelation	11
Deuteronomy	15	Psalms	102	10	Isaiah	42	Revelation	12
Deuteronomy	16	Psalms	103	11	Isaiah	43	Revelation	13
Deuteronomy	17	Psalms	104	12	Isaiah	44	Revelation	14
Deuteronomy	18	Psalms	105	13	Isaiah	45	Revelation	15
Deuteronomy	19	Psalms	106	14	Isaiah	46	Revelation	16
Deuteronomy	20	Psalms	107	15	Isaiah	47	Revelation	17
Deuteronomy	21	Psalms	108,109	16	Isaiah	48	Revelation	18
Deuteronomy	22	Psalms	110,111	17	Isaiah	49	Revelation	19
Deuteronomy	23	Psalms	112,113	18	Isaiah	50	Revelation	20
Deuteronomy	24	Psalms	114,115	19	Isaiah	51	Revelation	21
Deuteronomy	25	Psalms	116	20	Isaiah	52	Revelation	22
Deuteronomy	26	Psalms	117,118	21	Isaiah	53	Matthew	1
Deuteronomy	27,28:1-19	Psalms	119:1-24	22	Isaiah	54	Matthew	2
Deuteronomy	28:20-68	Psalms	119:25-48	23	Isaiah	55	Matthew	3
Deuteronomy	29	Psalms	119:49-72	24	Isaiah	56	Matthew	4
Deuteronomy	30	Psalms	119:73-96	25	Isaiah	57	Matthew	5
Deuteronomy	31	Psalms	119:97-120	26	Isaiah	58	Matthew	6
Deuteronomy	32	Psalms	119:121-144	27	Isaiah	59	Matthew	7
Deuteronomy	33,34	Psalms	119:145-176	28	Isaiah	60	Matthew	8
Joshua	1	Psalms	120,121,122	29	Isaiah	61	Matthew	9
Joshua	2	Psalms	123,124,125	30	Isaiah	62	Matthew	10

Reading Instructions:

The center column contains the day of the month. The two first columns contain the chapter to be read in the family. The two last columns contain the portions to be read in secret.

Robert Murray M'Cheyne's Calendar for Daily Bible Readings

July

They received the word with all readiness of mind, and searched the Scriptures daily.

Family				Date	Secret			
Book	Chapter	Book	Chapter		Book	Chapter	Book	Chapter
Joshua	3	Psalms	126,127,128	1	Isaiah	63	Matthew	11
Joshua	4	Psalms	129,130,131	2	Isaiah	64	Matthew	12
Joshua	5,6:1-5	Psalms	132,133,134	3	Isaiah	65	Matthew	13
Joshua	6:6-27	Psalms	135,136	4	Isaiah	66	Matthew	14
Joshua	7	Psalms	137,138	5	Jeremiah	1	Matthew	15
Joshua	8	Psalms	139	6	Jeremiah	2	Matthew	16
Joshua	9	Psalms	140,141	7	Jeremiah	3	Matthew	17
Joshua	10	Psalms	142,143	8	Jeremiah	4	Matthew	18
Joshua	11	Psalms	144	9	Jeremiah	5	Matthew	19
Joshua	12,13	Psalms	145	10	Jeremiah	6	Matthew	20
Joshua	14,15	Psalms	146,147	11	Jeremiah	7	Matthew	21
Joshua	16,17	Psalms	148	12	Jeremiah	8	Matthew	22
Joshua	18,19	Psalms	149,150	13	Jeremiah	9	Matthew	23
Judges	20,21	Acts	1	14	Jeremiah	10	Matthew	24
Judges	22	Acts	2	15	Jeremiah	11	Matthew	25
Judges	23	Acts	3	16	Jeremiah	12	Matthew	26
Judges	24	Acts	4	17	Jeremiah	13	Matthew	27
Judges	1	Acts	5	18	Jeremiah	14	Matthew	28
Judges	2	Acts	6	19	Jeremiah	15	Mark	1
Judges	3	Acts	7	20	Jeremiah	16	Mark	2
Judges	4	Acts	8	21	Jeremiah	17	Mark	3
Judges	5	Acts	9	22	Jeremiah	18	Mark	4
Judges	6	Acts	10	23	Jeremiah	19	Mark	5
Judges	7	Acts	11	24	Jeremiah	20	Mark	6
Judges	8	Acts	12	25	Jeremiah	21	Mark	7
Judges	9	Acts	13	26	Jeremiah	22	Mark	8
Judges	10,11:1-11	Acts	14	27	Jeremiah	23	Mark	9
Judges	11:12-40	Acts	15	28	Jeremiah	24	Mark	10
Judges	12	Acts	16	29	Jeremiah	25	Mark	11
Judges	13	Acts	17	30	Jeremiah	26	Mark	12
Judges	14	Acts	18	31	Jeremiah	27	Mark	13

Robert Murray M'Cheyne's Calendar for Daily Bible Readings

August

Speak, Lord; for thy servant heareth.

Family				Date	Secret			
Book	Chapter	Book	Chapter		Book	Chapter	Book	Chapter
Judges	15	Acts	19	1	Jeremiah	28	Mark	14
Judges	16	Acts	20	2	Jeremiah	29	Mark	15
Judges	17	Acts	21	3	Jeremiah	30,31	Mark	16
Judges	18	Acts	22	4	Jeremiah	32	Psalms	1,2
Judges	19	Acts	23	5	Jeremiah	33	Psalms	3,4
Judges	20	Acts	24	6	Jeremiah	34	Psalms	5,6
Judges	21	Acts	25	7	Jeremiah	35	Psalms	7,8
Ruth	1	Acts	26	8	Jeremiah	36,45	Psalms	9
Ruth	2	Acts	27	9	Jeremiah	37	Psalms	10
Ruth	3,4	Acts	28	10	Jeremiah	38	Psalms	11,12
1 Samuel	1	Romans	1	11	Jeremiah	39	Psalms	13,14
1 Samuel	2	Romans	2	12	Jeremiah	40	Psalms	15,16
1 Samuel	3	Romans	3	13	Jeremiah	41	Psalms	17
1 Samuel	4	Romans	4	14	Jeremiah	42	Psalms	18
1 Samuel	5,6	Romans	5	15	Jeremiah	43	Psalms	19
1 Samuel	7,8	Romans	6	16	Jeremiah	44	Psalms	20,21
1 Samuel	9	Romans	7	17	Jeremiah	46	Psalms	22
1 Samuel	10	Romans	8	18	Jeremiah	47	Psalms	23,24
1 Samuel	11	Romans	9	19	Jeremiah	48	Psalms	25
1 Samuel	12	Romans	10	20	Jeremiah	49	Psalms	26,27
1 Samuel	13	Romans	11	21	Jeremiah	50	Psalms	28,29
1 Samuel	14	Romans	12	22	Jeremiah	51	Psalms	30
1 Samuel	15	Romans	13	23	Jeremiah	52	Psalms	31
1 Samuel	16	Romans	14	24	Lamentations	1	Psalms	32
1 Samuel	17	Romans	15	25	Lamentations	2	Psalms	33
1 Samuel	18	Romans	16	26	Lamentations	3	Psalms	34
1 Samuel	19	1 Corinthians	1	27	Lamentations	4	Psalms	35
1 Samuel	20	1 Corinthians	2	28	Lamentations	5	Psalms	36
1 Samuel	21,22	1 Corinthians	3	29	Ezekiel	1	Psalms	37
1 Samuel	23	1 Corinthians	4	30	Ezekiel	2	Psalms	38
1 Samuel	24	1 Corinthians	5	31	Ezekiel	3	Psalms	39

Reading Instructions:
The center column contains the day of the month. The two first columns contain the chapter to be read in the family. The two last columns contain the portions to be read in secret.

September

The Law of the Lord is perfect, convicting the soul.

Family				Date	Secret			
Book	**Chapter**	**Book**	**Chapter**		**Book**	**Chapter**	**Book**	**Chapter**
1 Samuel	25	1 Corinthians	6	1	Ezekiel	4	Psalms	40,41
1 Samuel	26	1 Corinthians	7	2	Ezekiel	5	Psalms	42,43
1 Samuel	27	1 Corinthians	8	3	Ezekiel	6	Psalms	44
1 Samuel	28	1 Corinthians	9	4	Ezekiel	7	Psalms	45
1 Samuel	29,30	1 Corinthians	10	5	Ezekiel	8	Psalms	46,47
1 Samuel	31	1 Corinthians	11	6	Ezekiel	9	Psalms	48
2 Samuel	1	1 Corinthians	12	7	Ezekiel	10	Psalms	49
2 Samuel	2	1 Corinthians	13	8	Ezekiel	11	Psalms	50
2 Samuel	3	1 Corinthians	14	9	Ezekiel	12	Psalms	51
2 Samuel	4,5	1 Corinthians	15	10	Ezekiel	13	Psalms	52,53,54
2 Samuel	6	1 Corinthians	16	11	Ezekiel	14	Psalms	55
2 Samuel	7	2 Corinthians	1	12	Ezekiel	15	Psalms	56,57
2 Samuel	8,9	2 Corinthians	2	13	Ezekiel	16	Psalms	58,59
2 Samuel	10	2 Corinthians	3	14	Ezekiel	17	Psalms	60,61
2 Samuel	11	2 Corinthians	4	15	Ezekiel	18	Psalms	62,63
2 Samuel	12	2 Corinthians	5	16	Ezekiel	19	Psalms	64,65
2 Samuel	13	2 Corinthians	6	17	Ezekiel	20	Psalms	66,67
2 Samuel	14	2 Corinthians	7	18	Ezekiel	21	Psalms	68
2 Samuel	15	2 Corinthians	8	19	Ezekiel	22	Psalms	69
2 Samuel	16	2 Corinthians	9	20	Ezekiel	23	Psalms	70,71
2 Samuel	17	2 Corinthians	10	21	Ezekiel	24	Psalms	72
2 Samuel	18	2 Corinthians	11	22	Ezekiel	25	Psalms	73
2 Samuel	19	2 Corinthians	12	23	Ezekiel	26	Psalms	74
2 Samuel	20	2 Corinthians	13	24	Ezekiel	27	Psalms	75,76
2 Samuel	21	Galatians	1	25	Ezekiel	28	Psalms	77
2 Samuel	22	Galatians	2	26	Ezekiel	29	Psalms	78:1-37
2 Samuel	23	Galatians	3	27	Ezekiel	30	Psalms	78:38-72
2 Samuel	24	Galatians	4	28	Ezekiel	31	Psalms	79
1 Kings	1	Galatians	5	29	Ezekiel	32	Psalms	80
1 Kings	2	Galatians	6	30	Ezekiel	33	Psalms	81,82

October

O how I love thy law! It is my meditation all the day.

Family				Date	Secret			
Book	**Chapter**	**Book**	**Chapter**		**Book**	**Chapter**	**Book**	**Chapter**
1 Kings	3	Ephesians	1	1	Ezekiel	34	Psalms	83,84
1 Kings	4,5	Ephesians	2	2	Ezekiel	35	Psalms	85
1 Kings	6	Ephesians	3	3	Ezekiel	36	Psalms	86
1 Kings	7	Ephesians	4	4	Ezekiel	37	Psalms	87,88
1 Kings	8	Ephesians	5	5	Ezekiel	38	Psalms	89
1 Kings	9	Ephesians	6	6	Ezekiel	39	Psalms	90
1 Kings	10	Phillipians	1	7	Ezekiel	40	Psalms	91
1 Kings	11	Phillipians	2	8	Ezekiel	41	Psalms	92,93
1 Kings	12	Phillipians	3	9	Ezekiel	42	Psalms	94
1 Kings	13	Phillipians	4	10	Ezekiel	43	Psalms	95,96
1 Kings	14	Colossians	1	11	Ezekiel	44	Psalms	97,98
1 Kings	15	Colossians	2	12	Ezekiel	45	Psalms	99,100,101
1 Kings	16	Colossians	3	13	Ezekiel	46	Psalms	102
1 Kings	17	Colossians	4	14	Ezekiel	47	Psalms	103
1 Kings	18	1 Thessalonians	1	15	Ezekiel	48	Psalms	104
1 Kings	19	1 Thessalonians	2	16	Daniel	1	Psalms	105
1 Kings	20	1 Thessalonians	3	17	Daniel	2	Psalms	106
1 Kings	21	1 Thessalonians	4	18	Daniel	3	Psalms	107
1 Kings	22	1 Thessalonians	5	19	Daniel	4	Psalms	108,109
2 Kings	1	2 Thessalonians	1	20	Daniel	5	Psalms	110,111
2 Kings	2	2 Thessalonians	2	21	Daniel	6	Psalms	112,113
2 Kings	3	2 Thessalonians	3	22	Daniel	7	Psalms	114,115
2 Kings	4	1 Timothy	1	23	Daniel	8	Psalms	116
2 Kings	5	1 Timothy	2	24	Daniel	9	Psalms	117,118
2 Kings	6	1 Timothy	3	25	Daniel	10	Psalms	119:1-24
2 Kings	7	1 Timothy	4	26	Daniel	11	Psalms	119:25-48
2 Kings	8	1 Timothy	5	27	Daniel	12	Psalms	119:49-72
2 Kings	9	1 Timothy	6	28	Hosea	1	Psalms	119:73-96
2 Kings	10	2 Timothy	1	29	Hosea	2	Psalms	119:97-120
2 Kings	11,12	2 Timothy	2	30	Hosea	3,4	Psalms	119:121-144
2 Kings	13	2 Timothy	3	31	Hosea	5,6	Psalms	119:145-176

Reading Instructions:

The center column contains the day of the month. The two first columns contain the chapter to be read in the family. The two last columns contain the portions to be read in secret.

Robert Murray M'Cheyne's Calendar for Daily Bible Readings

November

As new-born babes, desire the sincere milk of the word, that ye may grow thereby.

Family				Date	Secret			
Book	Chapter	Book	Chapter		Book	Chapter	Book	Chapter
2 Kings	14	2 Timothy	4	1	Hosea	7	Psalms	120,121,122
2 Kings	15	Titus	1	2	Hosea	8	Psalms	123,124,125
2 Kings	16	Titus	2	3	Hosea	9	Psalms	126,127,128
2 Kings	17	Titus	3	4	Hosea	10	Psalms	129,130,131
2 Kings	18	Philemon	1	5	Hosea	11	Psalms	132,133,134
2 Kings	19	Hebrews	1	6	Hosea	12	Psalms	135,136
2 Kings	20	Hebrews	2	7	Hosea	13	Psalms	137,138
2 Kings	21	Hebrews	3	8	Hosea	14	Psalms	139
2 Kings	22	Hebrews	4	9	Joel	1	Psalms	140,141
2 Kings	23	Hebrews	5	10	Joel	2	Psalms	142
2 Kings	24	Hebrews	6	11	Joel	3	Psalms	143
2 Kings	25	Hebrews	7	12	Amos	1	Psalms	144
1 Chronicles	1,2	Hebrews	8	13	Amos	2	Psalms	145
1 Chronicles	3,4	Hebrews	9	14	Amos	3	Psalms	146,147
1 Chronicles	5,6	Hebrews	10	15	Amos	4	Psalms	148,149,150
1 Chronicles	7,8	Hebrews	11	16	Amos	5	Luke	1:1-38
1 Chronicles	9,10	Hebrews	12	17	Amos	6	Luke	1:39-80
1 Chronicles	11,12	Hebrews	13	18	Amos	7	Luke	2
1 Chronicles	13,14	James	1	19	Amos	8	Luke	3
1 Chronicles	15	James	2	20	Amos	9	Luke	4
1 Chronicles	16	James	3	21	Obadiah	1	Luke	5
1 Chronicles	17	James	4	22	Jonah	1	Luke	6
1 Chronicles	18	James	5	23	Jonah	2	Luke	7
1 Chronicles	19,20	1 Peter	1	24	Jonah	3	Luke	8
1 Chronicles	21	1 Peter	2	25	Jonah	4	Luke	9
1 Chronicles	22	1 Peter	3	26	Micah	1	Luke	10
1 Chronicles	23	1 Peter	4	27	Micah	2	Luke	11
1 Chronicles	24,25	1 Peter	5	28	Micah	3	Luke	12
1 Chronicles	26,27	2 Peter	1	29	Micah	4	Luke	13
1 Chronicles	28	2 Peter	2	30	Micah	5	Luke	14

Robert Murray M'Cheyne's Calendar for Daily Bible Readings

December

The law of his God is in his heart; none of his steps shall slide.

Family				Date	Secret			
Book	Chapter	Book	Chapter		Book	Chapter	Book	Chapter
1 Chronicles	29	2 Peter	3	1	Micah	6	Luke	15
2 Chronicles	1	1 John	1	2	Micah	7	Luke	16
2 Chronicles	2	1 John	2	3	Nahum	1	Luke	17
2 Chronicles	3,4	1 John	3	4	Nahum	2	Luke	18
2 Chronicles	5,6:1-11	1 John	4	5	Nahum	3	Luke	19
2 Chronicles	6:12-42	1 John	5	6	Habakkuk	1	Luke	20
2 Chronicles	7	2 John	1	7	Habakkuk	2	Luke	21
2 Chronicles	8	3 John	1	8	Habakkuk	3	Luke	22
2 Chronicles	9	Jude	1	9	Zephaniah	1	Luke	23
2 Chronicles	10	Revelation	1	10	Zephaniah	2	Luke	24
2 Chronicles	11,12	Revelation	2	11	Zephaniah	3	John	1
2 Chronicles	13	Revelation	3	12	Haggai	1	John	2
2 Chronicles	14,15	Revelation	4	13	Haggai	2	John	3
2 Chronicles	16	Revelation	5	14	Zechariah	1	John	4
2 Chronicles	17	Revelation	6	15	Zechariah	2	John	5
2 Chronicles	18	Revelation	7	16	Zechariah	3	John	6
2 Chronicles	19,20	Revelation	8	17	Zechariah	4	John	7
2 Chronicles	21	Revelation	9	18	Zechariah	5	John	8
2 Chronicles	22,23	Revelation	10	19	Zechariah	6	John	9
2 Chronicles	24	Revelation	11	20	Zechariah	7	John	10
2 Chronicles	25	Revelation	12	21	Zechariah	8	John	11
2 Chronicles	26	Revelation	13	22	Zechariah	9	John	12
2 Chronicles	27,28	Revelation	14	23	Zechariah	10	John	13
2 Chronicles	29	Revelation	15	24	Zechariah	11	John	14
2 Chronicles	30	Revelation	16	25	Zechariah	12,13:1	John	15
2 Chronicles	31	Revelation	17	26	Zechariah	13:2-9	John	16
2 Chronicles	32	Revelation	18	27	Zechariah	14	John	17
2 Chronicles	33	Revelation	19	28	Malachi	1	John	18
2 Chronicles	34	Revelation	20	29	Malachi	2	John	19
2 Chronicles	35	Revelation	21	30	Malachi	3	John	20
2 Chronicles	36	Revelation	22	31	Malachi	4	John	21

Reading Instructions:

The center column contains the day of the month. The two first columns contain the chapter to be read in the family. The two last columns contain the portions to be read in secret.

CONTACT US

Victorious Disciples
A
Ministry of

LIGHT OF THE WORLD MINISTRY
P.O. Box 1803
Cedar Hill, Texas 75106

To order additional copies of this book, for more information about
Light of the World Ministry or the Annual Victorious Disciples
Conference, please visit our website.

www.wandadavis.org

Victorious Disciples Leader's Guide Coming Soon

To order additional copies of

VICTORIOUS DISCIPLES

Have your credit card ready and call:

1-877-421-READ (7323)

or please visit our web site at
www.pleasantword.com

Also available at: www.amazon.com

Printed in the United States
81112LV00004B/19-26